Avery Press
New York • London

"HUDSON'S CHRISTMAS ON WOODWARD"
Closed for business 1983 • Imploded 1993

"For many of us, here is the one and only location of the 'true' Santa Claus and the magic of Christmas shopping. I combined the familiar with aspects of its earlier period. The viewer cannot help but experience flashbacks of the Salvation Army bell ringer, aromas of the cosmetics

department, glass elevator doors coupled with the elevator operators, and gold drinking fountains that made water seem elegant. Dining in one of the dining rooms was a very special event. For those that were there, these are sweet reflections." —Jim Williams, artist

SANDY RANGER
with Landon J. Napoleon

— Dedicated —

*to my five children (**bold,** in birth order)
and my thirteen grandchildren:*

Edward McDonald Ranger, Jr.
Sandra Devina Ranger
Stella Esperanza Ranger
Edward McDonald Ranger III
Michael Joseph Ranger

Patrick Arthur Ranger
Caroline Palmer Ranger
Gabrielle Kempton Ranger
Patrick McDonald Ranger

Julia Ann Adelson
Grace Ann Adelson
Thomas James Adelson
Barbara Shea Adelson

Jacqueline Ann Hutt
John Patrick Hutt
Julia Mercier Hutt

Peter Fall Ranger
Hattie Violet Mayes

My parents' wedding day.

− Contents −

— Foreword —

HOW, AND PERHAPS MORE IMPORTANTLY WHY, does one write her first book starting at 85 years old?

For me, the "how" was a fifteen-year journey that began in October 2004, shortly after moving into a residential community called Casa Blanca, a cluster of stucco townhouses replete with a 24-hour guard gate, three swimming pools, multiple tennis courts and a beautiful rose garden. A friend at our complex invited me to a party, where I met the woman who started the Casa Blanca Book Club in 1994. The night of the party, she invited me to be part of the group. The timing was just right. The busy chapter of my life raising five children was well in the rearview mirror, and two years prior, in November 2002, my second husband (we'll get to that later) had died. I was a widow with nothing but time, space and an open calendar.

One way I filled the lonely void was learning yoga in my early 60s, which was helping me become a more spiritual person. While yoga was wonderful, I couldn't spend an entire day in Downward

Dog. For many years I had enjoyed season tickets to the Scottsdale Center For The Performing Arts and the Phoenix Symphony orchestra concert series, but those events were better suited to attend as a couple. I needed more socialization and mental stimulation as I celebrated my 70th birthday in 2004. I'd always been a reader, and had been a member of two other book clubs—one in Michigan and another in Arizona—but as the owner of my own small business for thirteen years from 1984 to 1997, and a mother to five, reading time was often the first casualty on the calendar. Joining this book club would be a great way to meet my new neighbors, focus my mind and nourish my soul. I readily agreed to the book-club invite and decided my first meeting would be the December gathering, which would give me plenty of time to read that month's selection: *The Devil in the White City: Murder, Magic and Madness at the Fair That Changed America* by Erik Larson. Little did I know what an exciting adventure I was embarking upon—both immediately with that book and for the rest of my life as an enthusiastic reader—as I immersed myself in this true tale of the 1893 World's Fair and a cunning serial killer luring his victims to their death. Talk about a creepy page-turner! The combination of meticulous historical research and a nail-biting narrative kept me up late many nights. I was hooked, and I became a reinvigorated reader with that book. I finished the book much faster than I had anticipated, and eagerly awaited meeting the group for the first time.

In December 2004, about fifteen of us gathered for a Christmas book-club luncheon, which was a quick walk from my home. I loved every minute of it. These were all brilliant, engaging women. Yes, women: In the sixteen-plus years I've been a part of the book club we've never had a male member. We've invited quite a few husbands of the members, but none have joined us. And, boy, are they missing out! At that first meeting, the food was good, and the conversation was better. Sharing my own impressions of the book we'd read was wonderful, as was hearing different and varied opinions. It was very free-flowing, because we were discussing a subjective art—writing and the author's overall affect and ability to engage the reader and elicit emotions—so there were no right or wrong answers. Everyone's voice and input were equally valued. I could barely wait to get the next book, *The Lady and the Unicorn* by Tracy Chevalier.

From there I rarely missed a meeting. The Casa Blanca Book Club meets seven times each year, from November through May. We skip the three summer months and two in early fall when the desert heat is intolerable and many of our members seek cooler and less oppressive climes elsewhere. It's always a treat when we reconvene in November for our first book discussion of "the season" (like going back to school in the fall) and catch up on summer vacations and our children's and grandchildren's goings-on, and detail the latest health-ailment inventories. Yes, we are primarily a silver-haired lot enjoying the Golden Years, which is code for "the body ain't what it used to be." Sadly, we've lost a number of members through the years who have passed away. Others have moved away or moved on from the club. Despite the ever-shifting roster, we always manage to have ten to fifteen at most of our meetings.

Throughout the years, as I shared more of my own life experiences through the various conversations, I was often told by my immediate family, many friends, yoga students and fellow book club members that I should write down my own story. My immediate reaction was to dispense with that idea, because I'm not a writer, I said. In fact, I can't stand paperwork! So I never seriously considered even the possibility of penning my own memoir. Or, for that matter, that it would be interesting to anyone else.

Fast forward to early 2011; I was having a late breakfast with my son Patrick and his real estate partner. I shared with them that I was looking forward to my book club meeting later that day. My son's partner said he had a friend whose neighbor was an author.

Well, that's interesting, I thought. So, I asked, "What's the author's name?"

"Landon J. Napoleon," he answered.

"Wow," I said. "You can't make up a name like that!"

He told me he was going to get me a copy of one of the author's books. We said our goodbyes, and I didn't give it much more thought. A couple days later, on Thursday, January 27, 2011, my son Patrick handed me a signed copy of a book called *The Rules of Action* by Landon J. Napoleon. (I know the exact date because the author signed and dated my book.) I dived into the novel and enjoyed it immensely, because it chronicles the early career of a trial lawyer in Phoenix from 1970 to 1980, which had many parallels to my own life and my first husband (we'll get to that later, too). The book, in fact, was based on real events in the 1970s, which I always find enticing. I eventually took "The Rules of Action" to my book club and suggested it as a future selection, which ended up being our March 2012 meeting. In the book, the young lawyer takes on a nursing home conglomerate in a wrongful death case.

In addition to discussing the book over a chicken-casserole luncheon at a member's house on March 13, we had the special treat of having the author join us. Again, we were all especially impressed by his name: You can't make this stuff up. As an aside, Landon has since written the follow-up *The Dark Action*, which documents the same lawyer's life and career through the 1980s against the backdrop of the savings-and-loan scandal. The *Action* series chronicles the full arc of a lawyer's career, beginning in 1970.

Thus began an association with Landon J. Napoleon that led to my book club reading two more of his books. The next was *Burning Shield: The Jason Schechterle Story*, a true-life biography that documents the amazing story of a Phoenix police officer horribly burned in the line of duty who survives his ordeal with the love and support of his wife and an entire community. Both Landon and Jason came to the Casa Blanca Book Club luncheon on February 26, 2014, at Arcadia Farms in Scottsdale. They also brought two surprise guests: Rebecca Joy and Darren Boyce were two of the firefighters who helped rescue Jason from his burning patrol car on March 26, 2001, which was stopped eastbound at the intersection of Thomas Road and the 51 freeway. The luncheon produced an amazing and inspiring discussion.

Two years later we invited Landon back after reading his next book,

Angels Three: The Karen Perry Story, another true-life biography about a mother who loses her three children and ex-husband in a horrific plane crash into the Superstition Mountains east of Phoenix. Landon and Karen both came to speak to our group on April 13, 2016, at Paul Martin's American Grill on Scottsdale Road, and it was another touching discussion.

Despite my fellow group members and immediate family continuing to suggest that I write my own memoir—and my new proximity to an author with a name to behold—the idea of writing my own book had not yet taken hold.

Then in February 2019 my daughter Jackie introduced me to one of her friends who had just hired a ghostwriter to pen a memoir about her parents, who were immigrants from Argentina who had each earned their medical degrees in their home country and were looking for jobs. They got one job offer between them, in Nashville, Tennessee, and took a thirty-day boat ride to the United States, with little money and knowing almost no English. That story and the idea of writing a memoir fascinated me. That's when something clicked in my mind.

Finally, after a lifetime of being a reader and rubbing shoulders with published authors I'd invited, including Landon and Susan Pohlman (who came to our group and discussed her lovely book *Halfway to Each Other: How a Year in Italy Brought Our Family Home*), I warmed to the idea: What about writing my own story? I slept on it, and the next morning told my daughter Jackie I was determined to write my memoir. I asked everyone in my immediate family for title suggestions. It was my son-in-law, Tom Adelson (my daughter Julie's husband) who suggested a *Grace Fall Life* as the subtitle, which sounded just right as I was born Grace Sandra Fall. The nuns at St. Mary's Academy all called me Grace Sandra, but somehow when we moved to Detroit I just became Sandra.

Now I just needed to figure out who might be able to help me organize my thoughts and get everything down. I started with the two authors I'd met, had to our book club and enjoyed.

I called Susan first, and we scheduled a time to have lunch together to discuss the project. Then, apparently, fate intervened. Susan and I had to reschedule our appointment due to a conflict she had, and in the interim I talked to Landon, too, about helping me with the book. He was scheduled to start on another memoir for someone else, but that person had just called him and asked if they could reschedule later in the year. I decided to take advantage of that immediate opening. We started the process March 22, 2019. Susan was very gracious when I told her what I had decided, and told me that I was in good hands.

By the end of 2019, as we made steady progress on the book, doctors in Wuhan, China, were treating dozens of people beset with an illness caused by a new virus. Soon the entire world would know the new coronavirus disease (COVID-19) was being caused by severe acute respiratory syndrome coronavirus 2 (SARS-CoV-2). Landon and I met three times in January 2020 as Chinese state media reported the first known death from COVID-19, a 61-year-old man who was a regular customer at a "wet" market in Wuhan. The first confirmed case in the United States, on January 20, 2020, was the beginning of an unprecedented global crisis that would change all our lives.

In my corner of the world, the book I had waited eighty-five years to start would now require us navigating the logistics of a global pandemic to complete. Just months after the first documented case of COVID-19, we surpassed two million cases in the U.S., with more than 110,000 deaths. As we neared completion of this book it was clear the virus would claim more than half a million Americans.

During the same year, we collectively watched in horror the brutal killing of George Floyd on May 25 by a police officer, which sparked protesters to take to the streets in an unprecedented show of unity. In November we elected elected the 46th U.S. President, Joe Biden, and his running mate, Kamala Harris. In my lifetime I've witnessed major wars (World War II, Korea, Vietnam and Iraq); the 1960s assassinations of a president, his brother and Martin Luther King, Jr.; and Watergate, Black Monday and the 9/11 terrorist attacks. But these times in 2020 are unlike anything else I've lived through, with the collision of a global pandemic and a long-overdue uprising against institutionalized racism.

"Tough times never last, but tough people do!" said Dr. Robert H. Schuller, an American televangelist I would go to hear every other Sunday when my then-husband and I would alternate between Catholic mass one week and going to the then-called Crystal Cathedral in Garden Grove, California, to hear Dr. Schuller. Twenty years later, as we stared down a pandemic, that other question about the origins of my book became paramount: Why?

Throughout my life many people have told me I was, somehow, an inspiration to them. Without question, it has taken all these many years for that idea to sink in, that my story might be interesting and perhaps beneficial to others. And, at 86 as of this writing, I have more days behind me than before me. That is what brought me here, and I'm hopeful you enjoy reading about the journey as much as I have enjoyed living it.

—*Grace Sandra Fall Ranger*
Aka "Snady"
January 2021

"Age is mind over matter:
If you don't mind, it doesn't matter."

–Unknown

Mahatma Award

Sandy Ranger

BIKRAM'S YOGA COLLEGE OF INDIA
Fall 2003

— Prologue —

SUMMER 2003

"TELL ME ABOUT YOUR LIFE."

We'll begin this story with that line—stated by a benevolent, spiritual man who swept into my world and changed me, including the way I looked at everything in life. And then, just like that, was gone. This left me a newly widowed 69-year-old in August 2003, asking a vital question: What do I want to do with my life?

Some of my yoga instructors had the answer: "We think you would be a great yoga instructor."

Without hesitation, I said, "You know what, that is a great idea."

These were accomplished yoga teachers and spiritual practitioners at a studio where I practiced, so if they thought I was qualified, who was I to question their vast expertise and their assessment of my own potential?

However, most importantly, the reason I chose to tackle the nine-week Bikram training program was that I truly believed the practice worked. I had witnessed living proof, including fellow students who healed almost miraculously. One was a morbidly obese woman

1

who told me after class one day that it took her almost three years just to work up the nerve to come to a class, where she promptly positioned herself in the back row, in the corner, because she was so embarrassed. We all witnessed month after month as she stuck with it and consistently shed pounds, to the day she reached her goal of losing seventy pounds. A group of us from the class took her out to celebrate with a healthy lunch. I also watched a young man, who had been in a horrific car accident and was ravaged with scar tissue and barely able to walk, transform himself into a new person able to run in 3K and 5K races. Another case study was my accountant of forty years, who was scheduled to have a serious back surgery. I asked him one day if he had ever considered asking his doctor whether he could try a yoga class. The doctor said there was no harm in trying; just don't overdo it. In the end, my accountant was able to cancel his surgery and has not had any back issues since then, thanks to yoga.

ON that day my instructors planted the seed, I left the studio, stepping back out into the blazing August humidity of metropolitan Phoenix, climbed into my Lexus SUV—with the personalized plate "SNADY" I'd had since 1984 (one of my granddaughters will explain that later)— drove to my house in Scottsdale and immediately called Bikram Yoga world headquarters in Los Angeles. The woman on the phone was pleasant, and said she would email me an application form. I thanked her, hung up and thought: *The nice thing about the unknown is you don't know what you're getting into.* And, boy, was I stepping into the unknown!

Within a day, I had completed and returned the form and sent a deposit check for Bikram Yoga teacher training, which was going to cost me about $12,000 for the class time and $3,000 for accommodations. A few days later, a woman called back from Bikram to give me my housing choices. She said there were two options. The less-expensive option was a condominium arrangement that would include three other people. Or I could pay a little more and be on my own in a studio. I asked her to give me a little time to decide. While I was all-in on meeting other people, I also didn't know who I might end up with as my roommates for nine weeks. It didn't take me long to call her back.

"OK," she said, "I'll set you up in an individual studio by yourself."

"That's wonderful," I said, growing more energized by the minute. From there we finalized all the arrangements. I hung up, eager to do this training and anxious that I was wholly unprepared. She'd just told me most prospective teachers had received the "Authorized Teacher's Dialogue"—a forty-four-page, 8.5 x 11 booklet, laminated and bound with a black plastic coil—six months prior to training so they could learn and practice the script at home. Each teacher would have to recite the narrative word-for-word for each of the twenty-six Bikram postures. I, on the other hand, had jumped into this fire on a whim and only received my dialogue book a few weeks before I was set to arrive in California. When I cracked the manual open for the first time and realized I was going to have to memorize forty-four pages of material, I panicked. Here's one passage from the #1 pose, standing deep breathing Pranayama series:

Please listen carefully.
Inhale by the nose and exhale by the mouth.
Inhale and exhale should be through the throat.
Breathe as much as possible, as long as possible,
as slow as possible.
Breathe in by the nose, and out the mouth,
but all the time through the throat.
Nose and mouth are only passageway.

I knew I would be tested against that exact script. So, taking the last line above: If I said "Nose and mouth are the only passageway," i.e., merely adding an innocent article, that would be unacceptable and earn me a red mark. So, weeks before my adventure officially began, I immersed myself in that dialogue. That spirit fit with beliefs that had propelled me through almost seven decades: Keep a positive attitude, and enjoy what you're doing. It was going to be an anchoring principle that would be key in getting me through the next nine weeks... which began in a very mysterious way.

THERE were 276 of us gathered in the large Los Angeles studio, awaiting our guru to make his grand entrance. Staff had carefully arranged the four white satin pillows at the front where His Royal Highness would sit. We had each paid a hefty sum to be here, which infused the room with a certain energy, a combination of eager anticipation and nervousness. This was 2003, when Bikram Choudhury, who had grown up in one of India's poorest states, still held a mystical sway over his loyal followers. He had moved to Los Angeles in the early 1970s and set up his first hot yoga studio three years later. Bikram turned his unique take on yoga into a global empire that included more than 700 Bikram Yoga studios in more than 200 countries. By the time I showed up, he was wildly rich and had cemented his celebrity status along the way. That is, before it all crumbled later. Yet, at the height of his popularity Bikram reportedly earned almost $7 million a year. Before any fissures had appeared in his empire, we were all there to learn directly from the master. Once certified, we could return to our local studios around the country and lead our own classes in rooms kept at a sizzling 110 degrees Fahrenheit, or open our own studio if approved by Bikram himself.

I had boarded my flight in Phoenix on Sunday, September 14, 2003, for the one-hour flight to Los Angeles. I had no idea what lay ahead for me over the next nine weeks, which would be a bizarre combination of celebrity idolatry, Hindu mysticism, sleep deprivation, military boot camp, stress inoculation and exercising in a crockpot set to HIGH. I would be staying at Oakwood Apartments in Marina del Rey and commuting each day to Bikram Yoga world headquarters, which could be up to an hour away by shuttle bus, depending on traffic. The center was located on La Cienega Boulevard, which was six lanes across and bordered on both sides by single-story businesses, including a donut shop, a drive-through liquor mart, a Chinese restaurant and a tire shop. A few wispy trees dotted the sidewalk with their trunks covered by thick iron grates, their roots encased in concrete. My first impression, because it was devoid of any spiritual energy, nature or even a small swatch of grass, was that this was an oddly urban setting for a nine-week yoga retreat. I had been picturing more of a Japanese Zen garden atmosphere with the sound of trickling water, pebble paths and students meditating on smooth teak benches.

Inside, we all checked in and then sat waiting in a large auditorium-sized room. There was a palpable buzz of anticipation, as if the official program materials had listed Jesus Christ or Buddha as our program leader. When Bikram himself finally walked in, the room fell silent. He was smaller than I expected, and sported his trademark bald head and long braid. He wore only shiny black Speedos-type men's swimwear. He perched himself on his white satin pillows with the air of a monarch taking his rightful position on the throne. Of course, at the time Bikram was a celebrity worldwide, and there was not yet even a whisper of the scandal, criticisms and lawsuits from women claiming Choudhury had sexually harassed and assaulted them.

After greeting us, he asked everyone to give their name, state where they were from and tell why they had come to learn Bikram Yoga. As we began that process I looked around thinking, *This alone will take one of the nine weeks, because there are 276 people in the room. However, as people started to introduce themselves, my original eager anticipation turned to dread. If I took a quick assessment, I was in a room of people who were all on the younger side of life.*

"Hi, I'm Mike Woods. I'm 33 and here from Nashville, Tennessee. I'm a physician who regularly recommends yoga to my patients. I want to teach because I believe in the practice as a way of healing ourselves."

"Hi, I'm Jennifer Smith. I just turned 19. I live in Boise, Idaho. I begged my parents to pay for this course because I want this to be my career. I feel this is, like, my purpose."

"I'm Heather Long. I just turned 40 and I'm from Newport Beach. I'm quitting my career as a high school science teacher because I want to teach yoga now."

"I'm Morgan Agate. I'm 19, too, and grew up right here in L.A. I can't wait for this journey with all of you. Thank you."

I frantically but discreetly scanned the room to confirm the reality: Yes, I was indeed a 69-year-old woman surrounded by people decades younger than I, including some who were still teenagers!

Wow... I am way out of my element.

I had never thought of myself as being old, but... oh, shit! This was bad. I carefully eyed every door marked with a red EXIT sign and wondered how I might tiptoe away, sneak out the back and never return. Even the door closest to me would still require an embarrassing interruption, as I counted all the rows of people I'd have to navigate. Regardless, I decided that thirty seconds of anonymous embarrassment was the lesser of two evils: I certainly wasn't going to sit here and identify myself as the Official Cryptkeeper, born in 1934— just seven years after the invention of the first television. No way that was happening!

As the fifth student spoke, a stunning brunette in spandex who said she was turning 21 the next day, which explained her body that defied the laws of physics, I started to push myself up for The Great Escape. Would I get my $15,000 back? I didn't care: I'd pay a second fifteen grand to get out of this with my dignity. I wasn't going to humiliate myself for any amount of money. But before I fully stood to leave, the pony-tailed man, the anointed one, spoke from atop his pillows.

"Yogis don't have an age," he said. "I don't care about your age. Stop telling us how old you are. Age is mind over matter: If you don't mind, it doesn't matter."

Thank you, Mark Twain! Saved by the bell. And, of course, I had to concur with the little bikini-clad Indian man, who was only ten years younger than I was: Age was just a number. I'd lived my entire life with that belief. I settled back in, no one aware that I had nearly just bolted from the room like some senile woman, and I fully relaxed. From there, I actually enjoyed hearing the rest of the introductions, minus anyone's age. Once we'd gone around and gotten to everyone— Hi, I'm Sandy from Scottsdale, Arizona, and I'm thrilled to be here to start this journey of self-discovery—Bikram said we would officially begin that journey the next morning.

The next day we huddled at Oakwood Apartments under hazy skies and awaited the bus that would take us into Los Angeles. We were all chatting about how excited we were to begin this journey. There was nothing in the world I wouldn't try, and I loved challenges. At age 69, I knew this was going to be a challenge.

Boy, was that an understatement.

We would be doing two ninety-minute yoga classes each day, for a total of ninety-nine sessions over the nine weeks. Our eleven classes each week—two each Monday through Friday, and one on Saturday morning—were all in a room set to 110 degrees. Bikram himself would only be teaching three or four of the eleven classes, depending on the week. This was an exciting time when Bikram Yoga was all the rage, because his unique twenty-six posture class really worked. Between classes we'd see celebrities walking to and from the other studios in the building. At first, we were all star-struck: There's Meg Ryan! I saw Serena Williams and George Hamilton, with his trademark tan. One day I saw Robert DeNiro at the pharmacy and said to him, in my best *Taxi Driver* impersonation, "Are you looking at me? Are *you* looking at *me*?" OK, I didn't really say anything to any celebrity, but what fun it all was. But the yoga training was beyond difficult.

Thankfully, even as a 69-year-old widow, I was not truly an oddity in this wonderfully diverse confluence of people. We had men and women, of multiple ethnicities, across an age range of 18 to 69 (yours truly). We had career professionals including doctors, dental hygienists, insurance agents, lawyers, nutritionists, sports trainers, school teachers and small-business owners. We had people in the arts: ballet dancers, actors, aspiring filmmakers, other film industry types and everything in between. We had the very young just starting life straight out of high school, middle-age seekers looking for a new path, and even a few people clearly on drugs who had the time and money to be there on a whim.

Like a yoga version of the blitzkrieg across Europe, nothing stopped class. When one of the students started having an epileptic fit, they just hauled him out as though shuttling the wounded out of the trenches. Similar episodes happened twice, which prompted me to wonder why a doctor would pre-approve someone prone to seizures to undertake such a strenuous course. Both times, the other participants didn't even turn heads: Hauling out the wounded as we strained through poses was business as usual.

Each day began at 5:00 a.m. when the alarm went off. After a shower and light breakfast (you had to be careful what you ate, given the rigors ahead), I packed my meals for the day. It was always a rush, making sure I was outside to meet the shuttle bus by 7 a.m. in front of Oakwood Apartments, a vast sprawling complex. Most of us dozed during the ride.

Our first class, with all 276 people, ran from 8 to 9:30 a.m. in the 110-degree studio. With that many people sweating profusely for ninety minutes, the room definitely had an odor you'd never want to package and sell in a bottle. After a shower and lunch (which would turn into another daily oddity, as you'll see), our next class was 3 to 4:30 p.m.—i.e., sweat, shower, repeat. After dinner we broke out into smaller groups for testing. Similar to fraternity and sorority hazing, testing was always at night when we were exhausted. The instructor would call you in front of the group and say, "Posture number two." You had to demonstrate the pose while reciting from the Authorized Teacher's Dialogue, verbatim for that posture. Keep in mind, too, we had to recite these forty-four pages, through twenty-six postures, while concurrently contorting our bodies in the searing heat. My fear came back repeatedly, minute by minute, hour by hour and day by day: *I'm not going to pass.* And yet I would soldier on, surrounded by people twenty to fifty years my junior.

After testing there were early evening lectures. Depending on the day, we might hear from a nutritionist, a psychologist or a motivational speaker. While these speakers were mostly excellent, they were also inundating us with yet more information we had to attempt to process and retain as cumulative sleep deprivation whittled away our cognitive functioning. There was also the unending, looming dread of memorizing the Authorized Teacher's Dialogue, a prospect that circled us like a shark in bloodied waters.

Then, after each long day, Bikram perched himself on his white satin pillows and spoke from on high from 8 p.m. to midnight. That Bikram could drone on for hours and hours, night after night, was a monumental feat unto itself. And, boy, did he love to hear himself talk. There was no more pleasing sound in the universe, to Bikram, than the lovely strains and eloquence of his verbosity. He'd break out into song, too. We came to realize that he would do this *every* night after we'd all wrung every last drop of perspiration from our bodies and exhausted our minds by endlessly reciting that script. After the long drive back to Oakwood Apartments, it was usually around 1 a.m. by the time we were dragging ourselves off the shuttle bus, dreading the specter of the cruel torture device, which was the ringing alarm that would start it all over again in four or five hours.

During the first week, adrenaline and excitement fueled us through the challenge. By the end of the second week, everyone was starting to feel blunted by sleep deprivation. That's when we all started marking our calendars, with an "X" to cross off another completed day. By the third and fourth week, people started to crack and drop out. During testing, when a student didn't pass, they often burst into tears. Basic combat training in the U.S. Army lasts ten weeks; this yoga crucible would last nearly as long. From Day One, I told myself I could grumble and complain, but that was never my MO. I knew if I went down that mental rabbit hole I'd never climb out. I cried as much as anyone else, but quitting was not an option for me. None of us had a clue at the outset how grueling this was going to be. I could only fall back on my inner mantra: This is a challenge, and I can do it.

Concurrently, as early as those first few days, I started to sense Bikram's worldview was a bit off. Of course, I was in lockstep with Bikram on his philosophy (and his proven sequence of twenty-six postures) that had spared me on that first day: Age is mind over matter; if you don't mind, it doesn't matter. But beyond that, something just wasn't right with this guy. Wasn't yoga a spiritual practice, a way to lose oneself and connect to something deeper? A giving practice based on humility? This guy, with his name and brand trademarked and plastered everywhere, seemed to embody the exact opposite of everything I'd ever learned about the practice of yoga. Then one day during our lunch break, he confirmed what I had sensed.

Bikram walked into the room where we were all eating. His mere presence triggered a ripple of respectful awareness that silenced us all. Everyone awaited whatever spiritual gifts he might be so generous to impart upon his impoverished minions. Instead, he silently motioned us all outside, where we circled around his 1926 Bentley as he spoke of it in loving terms as though it were a living, breathing being he had birthed and nurtured himself. I only had one thought: *Who cares about your car?*

Thereafter, each day at lunch Bikram repeated the ritual by making us all gather outside to stare at another one of his dozens of classic cars. Years later, in late 2016 as part of a sexual harassment lawsuit, a superior court judge in Los Angeles would document forty-three cars in Choudhury's prized antique collection. In the judge's order, he stated that none of the vehicles could be removed from the state, including eight Bentleys, eleven Rolls-Royces, five Mercedes-Benzes, two Jaguars and three Ferraris, among others. While our frequent trips outside for forced fawning over his vehicles were weird, materialistic and narcissistic, it was all relatively harmless. So the guy had piles of money and liked his cars; that didn't mean he couldn't teach me how to become a good yoga instructor and, hopefully, a better person. But then it got worse over time, and even kind of creepy.

When he gave his hours-long diatribe each night, when all we wanted to do was get some sleep, he'd ask, "Who'd like to brush my hair while I'm speaking?" The first time he said that I was appalled that more hands than I could count went up. The younger women, specifically, were practically tripping over each other to go brush this odd little man's raven locks.

How degrading!

And so, while he rambled on for hours about God-knows-what—because we were all dutifully fighting off the overwhelming urge to sleep and not processing any of what he said—several young women (it was always girls in their teens and twenties) would take turns brushing his hair like slaves to the master. We knew our guru had a misguided materialistic affection for his forty-three classic cars. And now, I realized, public grooming rituals that demeaned participants who had paid to be there. Bikram would have been buried alive in the age of "Me Too" and "Time's Up."

It all struck me as a deep self-esteem gap, that this "spiritual" man had to be fawned over and admired for his monetary wealth. All combined, my perception of Bikram started to turn and subsequently made me question his true motives. But despite it all, I was determined to focus on my own journey—to grow spiritually, complete the course and help my future students with what I'd learned. Yoga is such a wonderful practice, and so good for the mind, body and soul. And, of course, I would not drag my own students out to the parking lot to admire my Lexus SUV, which was no Bentley but a vehicle I quite liked.

Mercifully, each week after our Saturday morning yoga class we got the rest of the weekend off until the indoctrination started again early Monday morning. Those blissful hours, our only free time the entire week, were as sacred to us as a weekend pass to sailors who'd been at sea for six months. I developed a pleasant routine that took me away from Bikram's oddities. Every Saturday, Barbara, a new friend I'd made from Washington state who had a car, and I would go do our early yoga class, go to Good Earth for a scrumptious breakfast and then go shopping at Whole Foods for our groceries for the week. And then we each treated ourselves to a two-hour Thai massage.

Despite the challenges, and the increasingly disjointed culture Bikram had created around himself, I somehow survived the weeks and eventually was at the precipice of actually passing. All I had to do was survive my final examination. I cannot overstate the Herculean challenge I had survived at 69 years old: eleven yoga classes each week (ninety-nine total) in classrooms baking us at 110 degrees. We existed on less than five hours of sleep a night for those nine straight weeks. In our sleep-deprivation reverie, we suffered further cruel-and-unusual punishment, which was having to sit and listen to Bikram speak for hours each night until midnight, followed by the one-hour bus ride back to our lodging. As I dragged myself off that bus each night, bone-tired, I knew the day was not done. My yoga clothes, which had gone through seven cycles of being soaked completely in sweat and partially drying (during Bikram's daily lunchtime classic-car-fetish viewing party and rambling evening lectures), had to be thrown in the washing machine before bed. I'd finally tumble into bed knowing the alarm was set for 5 a.m.

The physically grueling routine was way beyond anything I might have imagined when I naively signed up. It was almost like a military boot camp with one mission: Can we break you? It was by far the hardest thing I had ever done at the time, and almost two decades later remains as my most difficult undertaking. (This coming from a woman who birthed and raised five children, and hiked to the bottom of the Grand Canyon and back up… *twice).*

Along the way, my much younger classmates were suffering equally. Our numbers slowly dwindled, as students got kicked out or dropped out, driven away by any number of factors: the physical grind, the daunting task of learning that damned Authorized Teacher's Dialogue, or Bikram's own twisted philosophical combo of Eastern mind-body harmony and wanton Western materialism. It was all enough to defeat some of the strongest and fittest among us. Out of the original 276 students, nearly thirty would not graduate. Every student I talked to was, as I was too, counting down the hours, minutes and seconds until the torture ended. Of course, I was the oldest person there, and by a long span. There wasn't even another student in their sixties. I might have had an easier go if I had instead opted to join the U.S. Marine Corps and gone to Parris Island for new-recruit training.

Miraculously, on November 15, 2003, I was able to demonstrate all twenty-six postures and recite the accompanying forty-four page narrative word-for-word. The journey that had begun on September

14 was over. My fears and potential embarrassment of being outed as a relic on Day One had evolved into a phenomenal personal success. I would leave there thinking, *I can tackle the world, I can be anything, I can do anything.* My daughters had called me and asked what I was wearing for the graduation ceremony; we'd all been instructed to wear black. When Julie and Jackie arrived the morning of graduation, they presented me with a gorgeous, four-foot pink feather boa to complement my attire. At the graduation ceremony four of my five children were there: Julie, Jackie, Edward and Peter. (Unfortunately, Patrick had an unavoidable conflict.)

Peter (L), Edward, Julie (L), Jackie and me.

As the final icing on the cake, after we'd all received our diplomas, I received the Mahatma Award, which was given to the most inspirational student. When Bikram called me up to the stage I may have strutted just a bit, with my wonderful boa making me feel like a true celebrity. I was definitely humbled and awed by the thunderous applause I received, which I never expected. I was overwhelmed by the recognition. I did not win this award because I was the oldest and had somehow managed not to die. Rather, I performed well during my assessment. I was overwhelmed by my accomplishment and almost in tears of joy (or relief) that I had crossed the finish line. After the ceremony, my family and I departed for Shutters on the Beach, in Santa Monica, for a celebratory dinner and wonderful evening. We all returned home the next day on the same flight.

Back in Scottsdale, I was so proud of what I had accomplished. When I was a 4-year-old girl, I had wanted to be a gymnast, so becoming a certified Bikram Yoga teacher was really something. I dived in headfirst and was teaching up to seven yoga classes a week, at several different studios. I earned $45 for each ninety-minute class. That first year of teaching, I made back all the money I'd spent on training, and more. At one class I started with an old joke I was sure would send everyone into fits of laughter.

"Yogi Berra's wife came home one day, and he asked in a gruff voice where she'd been. The wife replied she had gone to see *Dr. Zhivago*." I paused ever-so-briefly for dramatic effect before delivering the hilarious punch line. My comedic timing, I believed, was impeccable: "'Oh great,' Yogi said, 'What's wrong with you now?'"

Silence.

Not even a giggle or a little snort.

I quickly realized I had completely dated myself: None of my students were old enough to remember the film, nor did they have any clue who Yogi Berra was. My resiliency didn't let this derail me, not even for one second. I had already been thrown into the fire—almost literally, at 110 degrees for nine weeks—and come out the other side. I'd always relied on my sense of humor, too, and so had never taken myself too seriously. I just moved on with the class, making a mental note that I needed to update my material. Moral of the story: Know your audience!

As I began the next posture, my mind wandered to how far I'd traveled in life to that place of teaching yoga at 70, a journey with more ups, downs, twists and turns than I can fully recollect.

And with that musing, I thought about that spiritual, swept-me-off-my-feet man again, and all he had meant to me in those three short years we got to spend together. And of course I thought of the man I'd been married to for more than four decades, and our five children. It made me want to get it all down, to capture the time and sense of place and the energy of everything, to keep it all alive to live and breathe again. So that's exactly what I set out to do.

Tell me about your life.

Part I

BEGINNINGS

— Chapter One —

MY FATHER, MY HERO

WHEN I WAS FIVE YEARS OLD, I DIDN'T KNOW THAT I ALMOST NEVER WAS.

Nor would I have really understood, or cared, because I was one of forty-four million people on my way to "The World of Tomorrow," the 1939-40 World's Fair, in a propeller plane piloted by my hero, Frank Park Fall. My father always wore a faded brown leather aviator's cap with droopy ear flaps, an endearing look that imparted a Jimmy Stewart likeability. We always sat side by side in the small cockpit.

Tall, lanky and handsome, my father was a veritable Renaissance man: a pilot, hunter, fisherman and military veteran who had served in France as a pilot. He was born June 18, 1894 in Meadville, in Crawford County, Pennsylvania, near where my existence might have never begun, in the breadbasket of America. This was the farmer's heaven of rural Pennsylvania, where plentiful rainfall fed rich soils ideal for farming. For more than one hundred years, Pennsylvania farmers led the Colonies, and later the states, in food production. Twelve miles east of Meadville, which was the first permanent settlement in northwest Pennsylvania, near the confluence of Cussewago Creek and French Creek, my hero's mother (whom I was named after) drank the poison in February 1915 when my dad was 21. They lived on a farm that was unremarkable from every other farm. The day she decided to die by her own hand, she could see the Lyona Church from the property—and beyond that the great fields, greenery and grist mills along the streams.

The tranquil country setting and pleasingly temperate climate, however, did not impede a spiral into mental darkness. To borrow today's language, Grace Ada, born with the surname "Hotchkiss" in June 1872 in Edinboro, Pennsylvania, had mental illness and, likely, depression. Before that fateful day my grandmother had suffered the kind of tragic loss that helps explain her desperate state. After having two sons (my father Frank in 1894 and my Uncle Fred in 1897), my grandparents suffered the deaths of their next four children: Uncle Ralph Fall died as an infant in 1903; an unnamed aunt died as an infant in 1905; another unnamed uncle died as an infant in 1910; and ten-day-old Aunt Mary Elizabeth died when my grandmother was fleeing their burning home and tripped. The infant's head struck a block of wood, killing her instantly in December 1914.

It was the very next year, 1915, while her husband, William Otes Fall, a farmer born in 1870 in Mogadore, Ohio, was away from home that my grandmother took her own life. The newspaper headline and the beginning of the account of the day provided the macabre details:

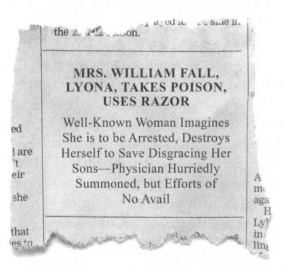

Mrs. Grace Ada Fall, aged 40 years [she was actually 42], *wife of William Fall, is dead at their home in Lyona, 12 miles east of Meadville, the result of a lethal dose of poison and also the opening of arteries under one knee.*

There is no possible doubt that the rash act was the result of a temporary derangement as indicated in the talk of the unhappy woman shortly before she passed away about 2 o'clock Thursday morning. When she was restored temporarily to consciousness she asked what had happened, and later she said that she had committed the act "because she was to have been arrested in the morning and she thought she might as well put herself out of the way and thus avoid bringing this disgrace on her sons." There is no evidence that the dead woman had ever committed any act for which she should fear arrest and it was evidently the product of a disordered brain...

Had my grandmother made this tragic and fateful decision some years earlier, before Frank Park Fall's birth, I never would have been on the way to the World's Fair in a plane piloted by him, my father. Likewise, had my father suffered the same fate of four of his five siblings, I would not be here to document my own eight-plus decades. In looking back at this chilling episode, I'm struck that our entire existence, and the subsequent intricacy of our family lineage, can be so tenuous and fragile. With just a slight shift of the cosmic tumblers, everything documented in these pages—my life and children and grandchildren—simply would not be. After his wife committed suicide, my grandfather William Otes Fall remarried Elsie Carr, who died in October 1930 at age 53, and then he married her sister Ida May Carr.

WITH his strong mechanical aptitude, my father moved to Detroit to pursue a career in the automotive industry. Dad got his early training at Ford Motor Company, which had been founded in 1903. Five years later, in 1908, Ford debuted the Model T and later developed new assembly-line methods in order to meet the growing demand for the vehicle. In 1911, before my dad joined the company, Ford established the industry's first U.S. branch assembly plant in Kansas City, Missouri. By the time Dad joined the company, he earned a $5 wage for an eight-hour day, which had replaced the previous rate of $2.34 for a nine-hour day.

Once he was living and working in the Detroit area, my dad met Ethel Catherine Fox, a Michigan native and self-professed "nervous Nelly" who, despite being born in 1894 in the Motor City at the historic dawn of the automobile age, never got a driver's license. Instead, she would get nervous even as a passenger, and pinch the arms of her four sisters. Her parents, my maternal grandparents, were both from Michigan, too: My grandmother Barbara Cecilla Ritter was born in 1869 in Wayne County, and my grandfather Jacob F. Fox was born in 1867 in Macomb County. I never met my grandfather; he died in 1919, fifteen years before I was born. By then we had already moved to Pennsylvania, and so likewise I never really saw my grandmother, who died when I was just six years old in 1940.

Ethel Catherine Fox and Frank Park Fall married July 10, 1917, in Detroit, when they were both 23. That they would remain childless for the next seventeen years was most certainly discussed in quiet gossip, the stuff of high scandal at the time. Yet this was not by some grand design: She just never got pregnant during all those years.

The same year my parents got married, Henry Leland and his son Wilfred founded the Lincoln Motor Company. The senior Leland had already cemented his place in automotive history as one of the founders of Cadillac, which he sold to General Motors in 1909 when my dad was fifteen. Leland named the new company after President Abraham Lincoln.

6644 Blakemore Street.

Meanwhile, by the 1920s Lincoln customers were having to wait up to a year to get a new vehicle, which put the company on the verge of bankruptcy. In 1922 the Ford Motor Company acquired Lincoln for $8 million, which is more than $120 million in today's dollars. Dad worked in that newly acquired division, producing the luxury models Lincoln and Continental. Built between 1917 and 1925, the River Rouge plant west of Detroit in Dearborn became the gold standard for assembly-line production. My father was there to help turn individual parts at one end into a finished car at the other. It was there that my father became an authority on the mechanics and service of the Lincoln model. Due to his prodigious skill base, in the 1920s Frank and Ethel moved to Pennsylvania where dad became the Lincoln Service Manager at Burnshaw Motor Company in Philadelphia. My dad later opened a Lincoln dealership on Chestnut Street in Philadelphia. My parents bought a narrow two-story building, an adjoined brownstone at 6644 Blakemore Street in Germantown. That is where my unusually older new parents—a 40-year-old father and a 39-year-old mother—brought me home after my birth on March 27, 1934. Decades later, in the early 2000s while visiting the area with my youngest son Peter, we went to find that childhood home, which we did. Seeing it again conjured so many memories as I saw the window to my bedroom on the second floor and remembered the train rides into the city. While I shared my memories with Peter, a woman drove up and parked in front of our old house.

"Do you by any chance live at 6644?" I called out.

She stopped, studied me suspiciously and shook her head without saying anything. Still in my reverie, I smiled and said, "I was born here and lived in this house about a hundred years ago."

Without missing a beat or betraying her poker face, she said, "You look pretty good for your age."

After she went into her own house next door, I ran onto the porch of my childhood home so Peter could snap a quick photograph.

WITH my dad immersed in the business of selling Lincolns, it was my mother who primarily raised me. In 1938, when I was 4, Mom squeezed me into my heavily starched navy-blue uniform to start first grade at St. Mary's Academy. Despite his busy work schedule, my father often walked me to school through crisp autumn mornings, brutal winters and the heavily anticipated arrival of spring each year. Back then it was an old schoolhouse with a total enrollment of eight children in the class. During the winter, after we trudged through the snow, the nuns would help us pull off our wet boots and then line them upside-down on the radiator, which would hiss and spit through all our lessons, including attempting to learn Latin.

With his success in the automotive industry, my father had acquired the means to buy his own single-propeller airplane, which he stored in a rented space at an airfield in Germantown. Every weekend, weather permitting, my father and I spent time together flying here and there for almost an entire year. These were short jaunts where we might fly to a nearby airport, drink a bottle of Coca-Cola and return home. Before I turned 6, I had more frequent-flyer miles than most adults.

Along with going to the World's Fair, he and I flew together to the 1939 Indianapolis 500. I have no recollection of that trip other than the little checkered flag he bought me, attached to a wooden dowel, which I still have more than eight decades later. My mother, meanwhile, who was terrified to climb in an airplane—and, as we've established, didn't even like to get in automobiles—always stayed home during these jaunts. That meant a particularly special time of bonding between a father and a wide-eyed daughter.

By the summer of 1939, although I was just 5 years old, I was already going to be starting second grade after Labor Day. The June Friday of our departure to the World's Fair "World of Tomorrow" (clearly my dad was able to get me excused from one day of school, as we would be flying into the future) was already warm in the early morning as my dad did his walk-around of the airplane and pre-flight checks. I gazed off at nothing in particular and took in the smell of fresh-cut grass around our small airfield in Germantown. We would be visiting the exhibits all weekend and returning to Pennsylvania on Sunday.

The fair had officially opened a few months before, on April 30, 1939, with 206,000 people jostling across 1,200 acres of exhibits at Flushing Meadows-Corona Park on a warm Sunday. Albert Einstein was on hand to give a speech that he began with, "If science, like art, is to perform its mission totally and fully, its achievements must enter not only superficially but with their inner meaning into the consciousness of people." The date coincided with the 150th anniversary of George Washington's inauguration as the first president of the United States. The fair would be open for two seasons in 1939 and 1940, from April to October each year.

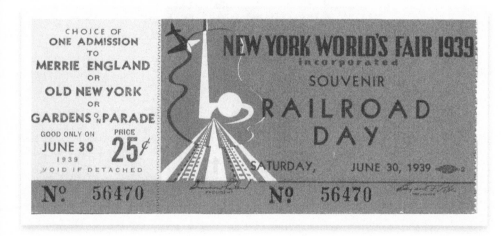

By the time my dad and I descended to Essex County Airport in New Jersey, the nearest airport for our smaller craft, I was overwhelmed by the excitement of what we were doing. And admittedly I was feeling a little grown up, even at 5 years of age. From there we took a one-hour car ride east to the New York City borough of Queens. For two full days, on Friday and Saturday, my dad and I strolled hand in hand, marveling together at what we were seeing. In the RCA Pavilion, we studied a sparkling and curious new invention being rolled out to the mass public for the first time: television. Just one of the many technological innovations on display; organizers had televised

President Franklin D. Roosevelt's speech during the opening ceremony to one thousand or so people lucky enough to have televisions in the New York City area.

Inside the RCA Pavilion, my dad and I could not stop staring at those flickering boxes, which were grainy black-and-white television sets with five- and twelve-inch tubes. We especially marveled at the television set with a transparent case, designed by RCA engineers to convince skeptical visitors that what they were seeing was not some deceptive slight-of-hand gimmickry. My dad and I were there, at the dawn of television, as the new sets soon became available for public purchase at stores in the New York City area. We also visited the exhibit featuring a Westinghouse Time Capsule, which is not to be opened for five thousand years, which will be the year 6939.

"I am enough of an artist to draw freely upon my imagination. Imagination is more important than knowledge. Knowledge is limited. Imagination encircles the world."

–Albert Einstein

Shady

My dad and I witnessed other new technologies being rolled out, including the introduction of the first fluorescent light and fixture. About a year after the fair concluded, the original three players in the lighting industry—Artcraft Fluorescent Lighting Corporation, Globe Lighting and Lightolier—began large-scale manufacturing of the fluorescent light fixture. By the time Dad and I took the ride back to the airfield and climbed in the airplane on Sunday, our feet were throbbing from all the endless walking. But we were inspired, too, by what we'd seen. As we eventually rumbled down the runway and surged into the gloaming, my heart was filled with a joy I could not have described then. I was just 5, and could not have known that this would be our last adventure.

BY spring 1940, my dad was a shell of his former self. He was sick with tuberculosis that would keep him mostly bedridden for the next ten months. At some point he ended up at a veteran's hospital in Castle Point, New York, where my mom rarely left his bedside. That was a lonely year for me, 1940, consumed by my dad's illness and my mother's absence. Certainly my mother's vast network of friends in Philadelphia had stepped in to watch after me so I could stay in school. I remember walking past a newspaper box in the city and seeing a headline that our grand event, the World's Fair, had officially closed permanently on October 27, 1940. I remember feeling happy that Dad and I would forever be two of the forty-four million people who had attended the exhibits marking the "Dawn of a New Day." And then I felt a deep sadness, too, that we had never again taken to the skies. My father no longer had the strength to get out of bed, let alone to pilot an aircraft with his only child as unofficial co-pilot.

My father, Frank Park Fall, died January 13, 1941, in Duchess, New York, two months before I turned 7. He was just 46 years old. I don't remember the day specifically, nor the funeral we had in Philadelphia where he had spent a good portion of his young life.

But I do remember the feeling of him being gone, which meant we would never again embark on another of our wonderful, windswept adventures. Instead, I was earthbound and headed east as my mother and I moved to Detroit.

— Chapter 2 —

MY MOTHER AND THE MOTOR CITY

WITHIN MONTHS OF MY FATHER'S DEATH, we were already living in a new house in another state. Detroit beckoned to my mother because it was home base: her birthplace, childhood home and a city full of relatives including her seven siblings—four sisters and three brothers, which meant twenty-two cousins. We settled at 14191 Cedargrove Street in Detroit, which was within the three-block area where all my aunts, uncles and cousins lived, bounded by Troester, Rochelle and Seymour roads. Mother and I lived in a modest house with two bedrooms downstairs and a small porch in the back off the kitchen. There was also a separate upstairs with a bedroom, bathroom and kitchen. Eventually, after the upstairs sat vacant for many years, my mother decided to rent it out because we didn't need the extra space. We almost never saw the renters, because they had their own separate entry.

Our modest house with a shingle roof looked remarkably similar to all the other houses in our neighborhood, which was not fancy in any way, and that suited Mom just fine. She was not a spender, and never even bothered to get drapes. Even as a kid I thought it was strange that every night we were on full view to anyone passing our house who might look toward the front window. On any given night, passersby could have seen my mother, me or both of us sitting and listening to the freestanding radio that was our one and only home entertainment source.

In that era, I was an oddity as an only child with a mother but no father at home. But my dearth of siblings did not diminish my joy, because my twenty-two cousins were all nearby. For grade school I walked to Assumption Grotto on Gratiot Avenue, the main thoroughfare just blocks from our house. At school I was once again taught by nuns. When I came home from school one day with lice, Mom took me on the back porch and used kerosene and a fine-toothed comb to get the nits out, which hurt!

In June 1943, my 48-year-old mom married Herman W. Schneider,

47, a toolmaker, whom she had known prior to marrying my father. My mom changed her name to Schneider, and I kept the surname of my biological father. My stepfather was an imposing German man who weighed well over two hundred pounds. He was also kind, caring and good to me. Of course, he would never replace my own father, but when Herman moved into our house I never had any sense of resentment or ill will toward him. If anything, it was nice to once again be a family of three.

With my stepfather as the breadwinner, I don't remember Mom ever working outside the house. She did, however, have a knack for winning prizes. She entered the Westinghouse Sweepstakes, among five million other entrants, and won prizes five years in a row, including a clock radio. The statistical odds of that happening are almost incalculable. She also seemed to win all the time at bingo. Despite her frugality, Mom had good taste and always picked out fine clothing for me to wear. In the kitchen she had an affinity for pork chops, whether grilled, fried, baked or glazed. In an epoch before anyone had ever heard of cholesterol, we consumed pork chops as though they were the only available food source and as essential to life as breathing oxygen. I don't remember anything except pork chops, fried in an inch of thick grease.

For my part, I was enjoying a typical big-family upbringing, because there were always cousins around to play with. I was especially close to a few of my cousins: Marilyn Handel, Nancy Phillips and Diane Kramer, who is several years my junior.

In the summer it was swimming at the community pool, and games of hopscotch and kick-the-can well into the darkness; in the winter it was endless snowball fights until someone packed one too tight and launched a direct hit above the neck. We took family trips, too, with aunts, uncles and cousins to Atlantic City, New Jersey. Then it all changed again.

In October 1946 Herman Schneider died from cancer after three short years of marriage to my mother. Like my father, by the end he was a ghostly shell of his former self. He was in such poor health that

we had to send him away to a veteran's hospital where he could receive around-the-clock care. We received a Western Union telegram October 5 with the news we knew for weeks would be forthcoming. Surprisingly, life went on more or less as usual. Mom and I stayed in the same house, where we were buoyed by the support of so many relatives.

In 1947 I started as a freshman at Dominican High School, a private, Catholic, all-girls school on McKinney Street in Detroit near Alter Road. The school had been established in 1940 and would remain open until 2005. I, however, only spent one year there—because I saw how much more fun many of my good friends from Assumption Grotto were having at the coed Edwin Denby High School. If I transferred I would be able to go to football games, a fall tradition in Michigan. I also wanted to join the swim and field hockey teams. So for my remaining three years I made the move to the school on Kelly Road in Detroit, which we all just called "Denby," where I earned letters in

both sports for each of the three years I attended there. The namesake Edwin C. Denby was an attorney and former Michigan legislator. He had served as Secretary of the Navy during the Warren G. Harding administration, a lofty ascension that might merit having a school named after him. However, he was forced to resign his position, and narrowly avoided criminal indictment, for his role in the Teapot Dome Scandal. Denby died in 1929, and I never did quite understand why the Detroit School Board quickly voted to name a new high school after someone who had been embroiled in scandal. After settling on an official name, the school board authorized the construction of the school and hired the design firm of Smith, Hinchman & Grylls before my mother and I had ever arrived in Michigan. However, in a strange twist years later, the CEO of that same firm was our neighbor on Grosse Pointe Boulevard when I had started a family of my own.

The school was completed in 1931, and its enrollment was 2,600 students that first year. A second addition to the school, completed in 1939 at a cost of almost $900,000, added seventeen additional classrooms, art and music rooms, "domestic science" classrooms (where we girls learned how to be good housewives), two machine shops, an auditorium with seating for more than 2,200, a large gymnasium with an indoor track, and a swimming pool. By the time I arrived, the capacity was 2,875 students. Our typical graduating classes had more than 800 students! At one point, Denby was regarded for a mathematics department that ranked high nationally. I loved being at the school because it was an exciting time.

Each day I entered the sprawling school, which was a three-story, multicolored brick structure. Like many buildings throughout Detroit, there were art deco stylistic elements on the facade of the building, including terra-cotta panels with custom reliefs designed and constructed by sculptor Corrado Parducci. Although I would like to claim otherwise, none of us particularly noticed Parducci's lamp relief, symbolizing the lamp of knowledge, nor his relief of a warship to honor Edwin Denby's naval background. Instead, we were busy being teenagers.

My days were full, and I got to know everyone. We navigated hallways and stairwells covered with terrazzo tiles. Brownish tiles covered the walls up to a height of seven feet, and lockers lined the walls. Our classrooms had wood doors and cabinetry. With all my good friends, we had a great time at all the dances and proms and in school clubs, and I dated my first boyfriend, Roland Eugenio (who died around 2010). We had a good football team, and the school had its own pool for swim season. Because I was two years younger than my peers, I was always lying that I was older. With that, I think I grew up a little faster because I was always projecting myself ahead. At this writing the school is still in operation with 500 students.

As I navigated the high school halls, a bit farther east in New York City, George Herman Ruth, better known as "Babe Ruth," appeared in uniform at Yankee Stadium in June 1948, as the team retired his number. He'd been battling esophageal cancer since being diagnosed two years earlier. My cousin, Walter Hotchkiss, an ear, nose and throat physician, was called to Ruth's bedside in his waning hours. On August 16, Ruth died of cancer at the age of 53. For two days following, his body lay in state at the main entrance to Yankee Stadium. Tens of thousands of people came to pay their final respects.

I graduated from Edwin Denby High School in 1950. Even though I was just 16, that September I was admitted to Hillsdale College in Hillsdale, Michigan, a two-hour drive east. My mother wanted to accompany me to college, and as our driver she enlisted her sister Barbara, whom we all called Aunt Honey. Once there I met my first roommate, who was the niece of one of the Ringling brothers who had co-founded the famous circus. It's not hyperbole to say that my first college roommate ran off to join the circus, because the daily grind of academia was far too pedestrian for her. I pledged the sorority Kappa Kappa Gamma and, to avoid the brutal Michigan winters, learned to play bridge. Perhaps it was prescient that for my first semester I took English 101, composition, in preparation for one day penning this memoir. I also took beginning Spanish, advanced shorthand, biology 101 and a PE class, hockey-basketball, which produced my only "A" for the semester. Two "C's" and a "B" in shorthand rounded out my report card for the term. For the spring semester I took English 102, advanced shorthand, advanced typing, office practice and business law, in which I earned a "D." I decided not to pursue law as a career, but that would not preclude me from marrying an attorney.

For my second year I took a number of economics classes, business English, Old Testament history and literature, and a class called "Meal Preparation." Yes, this was the early 1950s, when young women, in college or not, were groomed, trained, prepared and pressured to be child-bearing domestic engineers. The class was actually very helpful, as I learned for the first time that there were actually other home menu options and foods one could cook (and bake, grill and sauté) beyond pork chops.

After two years of college, by the time I was 18 and my Meal

Shady

Preparation skills were honed, I was ready to go to work in the big city. There was no financial impediment to my continuing, because my father Frank Fall had certainly left my mother in a solvent condition. And I enjoyed my classes at Hillsdale College. I was happy to have gone for two years, but I was ready to start my next chapter because I felt I was so wise at 18.

To launch my new secretarial career, I took a job I had found through the classified advertisements in the *Detroit Free Press*. From our house, I only had to walk a couple blocks to Gratiot Avenue, the main thoroughfare, where I could ride the streetcar to downtown Detroit. For my first day of employment, I ventured forth to the First National Bank Building, at 660 Woodward Avenue. When it was completed in March 1922, the twenty-five-story building was Detroit's tallest skyscraper. Five years later, on July 12, crews started on a twenty-five-story addition that would include a parking garage for eight hundred vehicles. Still standing today, the 750,000-square-foot building was bought by Quicken Loans co-founder Dan Gilbert in 2011.

On that breezy May morning in 1952, we had been enjoying a string of days with enough sun and warmth that I could finally leave my long overcoat at home. I walked to the streetcar in my black heels, climbed on and rode downtown to Woodward Avenue. The city was bustling with men in suits, ties and fedoras, and every woman was in a dress and shiny high heels.

Although I had already been there for the job interview, when I stepped into the grand lobby of the First National Bank building, one of the largest structures in the country, I was once again stunned by the long line of teller windows seemingly stretching on forever. Not wanting to be late on my first day, I decided that after work I would stop and count the teller windows: sixty-nine total! As people jostled past me, I turned and followed the flow to the bank of elevators, stepping off at the eighteenth floor to find my new employer: Rudolph Leitman New York Life Insurance. Rudy, as everyone called him, had joined New York Life in 1939 when I was barnstorming with my dad. By 1959, well after I was no longer working for him, Rudy Leitman would be the top agent in the country out of seven thousand agents. He was charismatic and wore a well-cut suit and a fedora. In his business he had no choice but to be outgoing, because no one was beating down his door to buy insurance.

Without knowing the wider context, on that first day as I walked through the office and met my new coworkers, I was indeed working at a top-notch outfit helmed by a talented leader. As the only secretary in the small office, I was always busy. I became quite proficient at taking shorthand, and the *tap-tap-tap* of my typewriter almost never stopped. That machine, emblazoned with "L.C. Smith & Corona Typewriters Inc.," helped us churn out endless letters to prospective and current clients, along with a similarly endless stream of insurance paperwork. For all my efforts I earned $34 a week, which I really thought was the cat's meow. In what seemed like a flash, two years passed. Although I don't recall why I left that job for my next post, it was an easy transition for a good typist who could take shorthand.

I next worked at the law offices of Bernstein & Bernstein, starting in 1953, in the same First National Bank Building on Woodward Avenue. Although I worked in a new job, my morning and evening route to and from work, via the streetcar that ran down the middle of Gratiot Avenue, was unchanged.

Mandell Bernstein was a first-generation American who attended the Detroit College of Law. After he established the firm, the successful legal practice represented labor unions, community leaders and businesses. Mandell became a Detroit icon of sorts, as a multifaceted leader in the legal, political and Jewish communities. During the 1930s and '40s, he and his brother David hosted a popular radio program in both English and Yiddish. At various times all four of the Bernstein brothers—Mandell, David, Nathaniel and Jacob—worked at the firm. Before I arrived, Nathaniel had already moved his practice to Indiana in the early 1930s, and Jacob died in his early 40s.

One legendary attorney at the firm was Estelle Koblin Nelson, who, when she attended the University of Detroit Law School, was one of two females in her 1936 class. When she was admitted to the Michigan bar she was one of only four women in the state to be members. Despite those accomplishments, her gender prohibited her from making court appearances. Instead, she worked behind the scenes doing research, writing and helping negotiate contracts.

To be a stenographer in a law firm from 1953 to 1955 was an introduction into a buttoned-up, conservative world where every thought, word and deed was carefully chosen and executed. I was in awe of being in such a prominent firm, and the way everything ran with such precision and scholarly decorum.

With that work background and my previous experience in the insurance world, I was ill-prepared for my next job, at just 23, in a much more freewheeling industry: advertising. While I liked working at the law firm, when I saw an advertisement for a similar position at an advertising agency, I was intrigued. I took an interview and within weeks had made the switch.

My third job in the big city, starting in 1955, was in an office located in another Detroit landmark: the Penobscot Building, which upon completion in 1928 was the tallest outside of New York or Chicago. That height distinction also made the forty-seven-story building the fourth-tallest in America and the eighth-tallest in the world. Named for the Native American Penobscot tribe from Maine, the building remained the tallest in Michigan until 1977 with the construction of the Renaissance Center hotel tower. I was, literally, moving on up!

Similar to when I started working at the First National Bank building, walking for the first time up to the Penobscot building, with its elaborate art deco style, had me in awe of the Indiana limestone that rose thirty stories from a granite base. From there the building had a series of setbacks topped with a red-neon beacon tower. Like many other art deco buildings, the "H" shape created more window surfaces to allow maximum sunlight into the work spaces. Each day as I entered the opulent property I admired the sculpture by the same Corrado Parducci whose work had adorned my high school. I loved strolling beneath the Native American ornamentation in the entrance archway and walking past similar metalwork in the lobby on my way to Kenyon & Eckhardt, a name everyone knew in Detroit. The advertising agency occupied two full floors of talented people and buzzed with an electricity that was palpable from Day One.

The firm started in October 1929 when two employees at a New York-based agency bought out the company Ray Lillibridge was selling. Otis Kenyon and Henry Eckhardt built their business throughout the 1930s. Kellogg Company, the breakfast-food proprietors from nearby Battle Creek, Michigan, became a client in 1934. By the time I was an airborne 5-year-old on adventures with my dad, Kenyon & Eckhardt was handling Abercrombie & Fitch Company, Munsingwear Inc., John B. Stetson Company and Quaker State Oil Refining Company. In July 1942, co-founder Eckhardt died at age 48. His partner Kenyon assumed the post of chairman, which he held until his death seven years later in 1949. The business grew to include Kellogg accounts (Bran Flakes, Pep, Raisin Bran, Rice Krispies and the golden goose, Corn Flakes) along with other household brands: Wesson Oil, Morton Salt, Borden Company and Pepperidge Farm. In March 1948, Kenyon & Eckhardt landed the business of Ford Motor Company ("Ford has a better idea") and, soon thereafter, Ford's Lincoln-Mercury, an important brand in my late father's own career decades earlier and the foundation of our family in the 1930s. In March 1954, Kenyon & Eckhardt won the Radio Corporation of America account and, the next year, launched a campaign touting the first color television sets to the U.S. market; agency billings reached $68 million in 1955. I had been there at the dawn of television at the World's Fair, and now I was going to be in the business of promoting that same product to the wider masses.

Looking back, by my first day of work at Kenyon & Eckhardt in

1955, whatever culture the two founders had established gave way to, or was further fueled by, the hyper-sexism of 1950s advertising. Concurrently, somehow Kenyon & Eckhardt boasted an unusually large percentage of employees descended from a higher order of physical beauty and aesthetics. The men were quite stylish and dapper in their suits, ties and fedoras, with a precision flair I had not seen in the law and insurance offices where I'd worked. Beards were as rare as a warm January day in Detroit. With the short, tight haircuts in style at the time, the men always had a fresh, clean look that was an appealing default of the era. Thankfully, during my entrée to the workplace, we were still five decades away from men trying to impress—by attempting to appear as though they were not trying to impress—by walking around today looking like they just rolled out of bed and wrapped themselves in rags with saggy pants that somehow defy gravity by clinging between the backside and knees. My time in the workplace, from the mid-1950s to the early 1960s, may have been the last chapter of refined fashion worn by both men and women.

At Kenyon & Eckhardt the women, too, dressed for work duty as though they were stepping onto a movie set. They coordinated their outfits beautifully from head to toe, starting with their stylish hats (always removed once inside the office) that always matched the two-piece look favored in the day, a buttoned top and long skirt. The top piece was usually long-sleeve, with or without a collar, and buttoned all the way to the neck. That top was the same color as the skirt that stopped about four inches below the knee. The heels were always either black or white. The understated pulse of sexual energy came from the way the cut of the clothing, top and skirt, hugged the shape of everything on top and every curve from the waist down.

Everyone worked long and hard hours at Kenyon & Eckhardt and were not unlike the characters in *Mad Men*. I would diligently watch this seven-season series of ninety-two episodes five decades later and be amazed at the way the TV show exactly captured the creativity, the time and the cavorting with each other—during and after work—and the drinking—during and after work. The men and

*"Do not fear going forward slowly,
fear only to stand still."*

—Chinese wisdom

women alike were beautiful at Kenyon & Eckhardt, and all the men—single, married or in transition back and forth between the two—were chasing every employee in skirts and high heels. Although many of the men who worked there were married, you wouldn't know it by the way they pursued every young girl in the employ of the agency, including me. There was a clear correlation between the way the men acted toward the women and the advertisements Kenyon & Eckhardt and other agencies churned out. One print advertisement showed a woman on Christmas morning fawning over a new vacuum cleaner with the headline: *She'll be happier with a Hoover.* Yes, because there was no greater happiness than keeping a home clean. In another ad for Van Heusen shirts, the dutiful wife was on her knees (on her knees!) serving breakfast in bed to her husband with the headline: *Show her it's a man's world.* Indeed, it was: I was a twenty-something woman and secretary trying to navigate that man's world. Every day, I kept my head down, kept my typewriter chugging and dodged the unending onslaught of advances by married men who were already having dalliances with other women in the office. By today's standards half the lecherous men I worked with at Kenyon & Eckhardt would have been charged with sexual harassment, and the other half would be under investigation for the same charge. It really was the Wild West of Unchecked Male Impulses in the workplace. Somehow, they all got their work done; maybe the martinis fueled the creativity.

Perhaps some of that excess testosterone fueled the creative work, too. The advertising business was notoriously competitive, wildly unpredictable and difficult to sustain. My first year there we lost a pitched battle for the Coca-Cola account to mega-agency McCann Erickson. Then, just before Christmas 1955, we won the Pepsi-Cola account. That victory meant profit, new stability and a seventh-place ranking among U.S. agencies. Perhaps you're old enough to remember the slogans that came out of our product repositioning, taking Pepsi from a budget beverage to an upscale refreshment: "Be Sociable, Have a Pepsi" and "Say Pepsi, Please."

One of my favorite escapes from that frenetic world of pressure deadlines and unwanted advances came reliably, like clockwork, every Thursday at noon. Each week I would descend on an elevator to the Penobscot building lobby, where my mom would be waiting for me. To this day, I can still see her standing there by the bank of elevators in her coral winter coat with the brown fur collar as people hustled back and forth. She always smiled and waved in anticipation of our destination. We'd greet each other and then walk two blocks together to J.L. Hudson on Woodward Avenue. These weekly meetups were even more special throughout the holiday season, when festive decorations festooned the cityscape. We'd walk past the Salvation Army bell-ringers and take in the smell of roasting chestnuts. Inside the impressive department store we'd stroll through the sweet fragrances of the cosmetic department to the glass elevator doors, where a uniformed operator would ask our destination, which was the thirteenth floor.

The dining room at J.L. Hudson department store, was the place to go in the city, and we always tried to get a table by a window where we could watch busy Woodward Avenue below. Then we'd each order the famous chicken pot pie, with a rich and creamy filling that warmed us, and a flaky crust that was so delectable I can still taste its buttery perfection at this writing. If flying together was one of my most endearing memories with my father, with my mother it was sharing chicken pot pie at the J.L. Hudson department store in downtown Detroit, just the two of us in a timeless moment as the city whirled around us.

— Chapter Three —

MY HUSBAND

THE BUSTLING OPERATION, LIKE SO MANY OTHERS, was part of the collective birthplace of the automobile, an industry that encompassed the surrounding Detroit region and marshalled an army of bare-knuckled workers. It was executives at Chalmers Motor Company who built the huge plant in 1908. By 1925, as brands merged, Walter P. Chrysler reorganized one particular firm as the Chrysler Corporation. The factory, on the south side of East Jefferson Avenue at Conner, was aptly known as Chrysler's Jefferson Avenue plant and would churn out DeSotos and other models of automobiles until the early 1990s.

Not far from that busy factory was a typical lower-middle-class neighborhood, where Lena and Arthur Ranger lived at 1604 Cadillac Boulevard near Jefferson Avenue. Their house was a narrow, two-story beige brick structure. They had married in Ontario, Canada, in 1910. By the time they emigrated to America, they had eight children in tow. Their ninth and final child, Edward McDonald Ranger, was the only one of his siblings born (October 15, 1929) in the U.S.A., in Detroit. Ned, as his family took to calling him from an early age, emerged into the world in the middle of the Wall Street Crash of 1929, which had started September 3. Then, nine days after Ned was born, a series of days tagged with the "Black" moniker ushered in the Great Depression: Black Thursday (October 24), Black Monday (October 28) and Black Tuesday (October 29). By 1932, when Ned was just 3, the U.S. stock market finally reached its low—down eighty-nine percent from its highest point. With a start in life like that, there was nowhere for Ned to go but up.

While the collapse of prices on the New York Stock Exchange was a seminal historical event, Arthur and Lena Ranger were more preoccupied with feeding, clothing and raising nine children. Arthur was a carpenter. Lena had the heavier workload as a stay-at-home mom with enough children to field an all-Ranger baseball team. The Catholic household revolved around work and church schedules, and every Sunday a hot pot roast came out of the oven with bowls of buttery vegetables and mashed potatoes.

When Ned was just 11, his father died. By high school, Ned somehow already knew he wanted to be a lawyer, which was going to be a daunting undertaking coming from his modest beginnings. But Ned had a plan, and he was up for any arduous task. While all his classmates at Detroit Catholic Central High School slept, Ned crawled out of bed every weekday morning at 4 a.m. After getting dressed, he walked to Chrysler's Jefferson Avenue plant to start work by 5 a.m. These early-morning walks through the Arctic darkness were especially brutal during the hard-bitten winter, which in Detroit seemed to last from Halloween to the end of school in June.

Inside the factory, Ned donned a stained white apron and went to work cooking breakfast for the shift workers alongside a crew made up entirely of men. The tenacious, personable and intelligent high school kid held his own amid the gruff banter of the unshaven and sometimes unsavory. In his own way, Ned was part of the rich history and tradition of the Motor City as the great automotive machine churned out vehicles. As the men came off the night shift, with fingertips blackened and knuckles bloodied by a night on the assembly line, they wolfed down the eggs, bacon and toast cooked by Ned and the others. After cleanup, Ned stripped off the apron and then had to hustle to get to Catholic Central High School on time, a journey that required taking two different city buses. It's difficult to imagine any modern-day teenager following a similar daily routine. He graduated from Catholic Central in 1947.

From 1947 to 1951 Ned worked different jobs. Then in 1951 he launched the next phase of his careful plan, which was to serve in the military—as a means to attend college. Ned enlisted and served in the U.S. Air Force from April 1951 to December 1952. His journey began at Lowry Air Force Base, located about six miles southwest of Denver, for eight weeks of basic training. He then served at Selfridge Air National Guard Base in Mount Clemens, Michigan, and Carswell Air Force Base in Ft. Worth, Texas. After he concluded his military service, Ned worked as a claims adjuster for The Hartford life insurance in Detroit.

In 1954 our paths crossed at a holiday party. For me there was an immediate intrigue. He was the smartest person I'd ever met. He was an intellectual with a serious focus, and he told me of his plan to become a lawyer. I told him I was working as a stenographer at Bernstein & Bernstein, and of course Ned knew the firm and even that it was located in the First National Bank Building on Woodward Avenue. Ned knew about our legendary attorney at the firm, too, Estelle Koblin Nelson, who was a local legend in legal circles.

I don't know that it was "love at first sight," or if such a phenomenon even exists. But there was certainly an interest and connection for us. Perhaps it was "love at a fairly rapid pace," because we started dating immediately. Initially, Ned definitely pursued me, and then, gradually, the feeling was mutual. Ned lived with friends on Cass Avenue and had a car. We both had good jobs, too: I at the law firm and he at The Hartford. We loved going out to eat. He took me to Joe Muer Seafood restaurant, which became one of our favorites from the start.

When we wanted a bigger splurge, we went to Driscoll's Steakhouse on Jefferson Avenue. A child of Detroit, Ned loved going to car shows, too, and we went often.

As our dating progressed, my mother—perhaps assuming the role of my father—approved of Ned only after close scrutiny. I only knew Ned's mom, as his father had died, and she was a kind soul. One night at dinner, at the Caucus Club restaurant downtown on West Congress, I ordered my customary Manhattan. Luckily, I didn't choke on the ring Ned had slipped into my glass. Less than two years after we had met, we got married, on January 21, 1956, on a typical icebound Detroit winter day.

Uncle Joe and me.

I was 21; Ned Ranger was 26. We had a small Catholic wedding at Assumption Grotto church, with about fifty people. Both of us had already lost our fathers, but both our mothers were there. My maternal

"The best and most beautiful things in the world cannot be seen or even touched. They must be felt with the heart."

–Helen Keller

Shady

Uncle Joe gave me away. We had our reception at the Whittier Hotel on Burns Drive near the corner of East Jefferson, on Detroit's lower east side. Later, in February, we would take a three-day honeymoon to Boyne Mountain Resort for a ski trip in northern Michigan. However, immediately after the wedding we went to live in a hotel to start our life together.

Built in 1926, the Belcrest Hotel on Cass Avenue was a twelve-story apartment building shaped like a "T" and sheathed with brick and terra cotta. In another example of Detroit style, the building had terra cotta cornices on the third, eleventh and top floors, emphasizing the horizontal lines. There were further embellishments with dentils, rope and acanthus-leaf molding, and green highlights. Although Ned didn't carry me through the entryway, it had wrought iron gates. This was a residential hotel catering to wealthy tenants, with a unique offering of amenities. We had daily maid service and a restaurant on-site.

Ned had been admitted to Wayne State University in September 1955, and our new residence was just blocks from the campus. University administrators admitted him under a special status on the basis of his military service and various letters of recommendation. The same month we got married, in January 1956, he started law school at the downtown Detroit campus. For the next three years, until 1958, Ned worked full-time as a claims adjuster at The Hartford and then took night classes Monday through Friday, from 6 p.m. to 9 p.m. I also was working full-time at Kenyon & Eckhardt and, since my new husband was in class, I decided to apply to Wayne State University as a regularly matriculated student and took two classes each semester at the same time Ned was attending his Monday through Friday classes, from 6 p.m. to 9 p.m. I was officially admitted to the university in January 1961.

In late 1958 we bought a house at 10761 Corning in Oak Park, a mostly Jewish community. Ned would drive me to Woodward Avenue, where I could catch the bus to Kenyon & Eckhardt. These were full days for us both as we worked all day and then went to classes at night. I was exhilarated by the busy routine and the excitement of

Ned being in law school. On weekends we explored Detroit and the surrounding areas. One of those outings was an invitation to a square-dance party from our friends Bunny and Dan Cooper.

"What's the attire?" I asked.

She responded, "Just dress the part."

My Hillsdale College portrait.

With that directive, I was soon at a costume shop, because for these sorts of events there was no payoff in moderation: I would go all out. By the time Ned and I were dressed on the night of the dance, I could barely squeeze into the car in my canary yellow skirt with an industrial crinoline cage rigid enough to contain two wolverines as house pets. The skirt was so big, in fact, I had to sit in the back seat of the car. We arrived, and Ned spent the next five minutes trying to pull me from the car. He had on a shiny black shirt, black slacks, a bolo tie and a silver belt buckle the size of a dinner plate that he'd polished to perfection. As we walked toward the venue, Ned strutted in his high platform shoes while I danced along in my lace-up ballet shoes.

When we stepped in the room, everything went quiet. We were the only people in such resplendent dress. "Dress the part" had, apparently, meant something simple. We stood out so much the entire crowd thought we were the official dance callers. I immediately felt sick to my stomach and grabbed Ned's arm. We were both mortified; the moral of the story was already bubbling up in my mind: Are we communicating properly?

ON June 11, 1959, Ned graduated from Wayne State University near the middle of his class of 88, and passed the Michigan State Bar exam soon after. Ned and Robert Sullivan subsequently founded their own firm, Ranger & Sullivan, combining their years of legal and administrative experience in the insurance industry. Richard Ward and Robert Sullivan Jr. joined the practice shortly thereafter, making it Sullivan, Sullivan, Ranger & Ward.

Edward

Patrick

TIME

MAN OF THE YEAR

PETER RANGER

Julie

Jackie

— Chapter Four —

MOTHERHOOD

I DID NOT KNOW I WAS PREGNANT when the relatively unknown, Harvard-educated World War II veteran announced his candidacy for thirty-fifth President of the United States in January 1960. By month's end, however, the world would know much more about John F. Kennedy, a U.S. senator from Massachusetts, and I would know I was going to be a mother for the first time.

These were good times in America, as fifteen years of post-World War II recovery and rebuilding reached its peak. There was a collective sense of common values—that what our parents had taught us made sense. We were still dancing and singing along to the carefree rock-and-roll from the 1950s, a full decade before Bob Dylan and Joan Baez held up a mirror to everything wrong in society. If we needed any evidence that our mainstream values worked, we only had to look as far as the ease of our daily lives.

Ned and I both had good jobs (although I would stop working in spring 1960 when I was pregnant) that had allowed us to buy our first home at 10761 Corning in Oak Park, which cost just $14,000 for the two-bedroom house on a corner lot. We had the only fireplace in the neighborhood. We could take to the open roadways fueled by gasoline at 25 cents per gallon. For dinner, I could stop at Kroger or A&P and get an oven-ready turkey for 39 cents.

Little did I know that this calm before the storm was the last hurrah of collective innocence before the '60s exploded into full-blown revolution, political upheaval, a horrific war in Vietnam and the assassination of President Kennedy. In March 1968, Martin Luther King Jr. spoke at Grosse Pointe South High School, which Edward, Patrick and Julie would later attend. Less than a month later, he was assassinated. On June 5, it was Bobby Kennedy. In stark contrast to those horrors, as I looked forward to being a mom at the beginning of the decade, Ned and I were blissfully immersed in the white-picket-fence American Dream.

He and I shared the same predominant emotion about the prospect of parenthood: elation! It had taken us a little longer than expected to get pregnant. Being an only child myself, I had always thought it would be the greatest blessing to have my own big family. The year 1960 was a fitting start to that journey—as the unknown idealist Kennedy made his case to replace a household name enjoying an average approval rating of sixty-five percent (Dwight Eisenhower)—as my firstborn would one day enter the political fray with his own bid for the U.S. Senate. But all that would come much later: First I had to survive the carnival ride of my body being pregnant for the first time.

The first trimester was similar to three months of one-too-many Manhattans at Joe Muer Seafood—minus the fun and seafood. At times, I was also ungodly tired: I'd feel energized one minute and the next minute feel as though I hadn't slept for a week. Each of my breasts had a mind of its own, and swelled to proportions that might have pleased Ned; however, even a slight breeze in a neighboring county was painful. Despite the distresses, the feeling of the fetus moving was an indescribable joy. There was nothing quite like feeling the nudges gradually grow in strength until the little one was hitting me regularly with unmistakable jabs. As Kennedy campaigned and Elvis Presley returned to the U.S. after serving two years abroad in the U.S. Army, my little one sparred with my belly.

I had a petite baby bump by May 6, which is the day President Eisenhower signed the Civil Rights Act of 1960 into law, which created penalties for obstructing voter registration and extended the life of the Civil Rights Commission that had been set to expire. Again, there was another parallel between world events and my own nascent progeny who would one day also champion equality and justice as a lawyer.

By the time the fastest woman in the world, Wilma Rudolph, was cementing her fame at the 1960 Summer Olympics—held from August 25 to September 11, her haul included two individual gold medals (100- and 200-meter dash) and a team gold medal (4 x 100-meter relay)—I was just days away from delivering my first baby. That the former polio patient who'd had to wear leg braces could win Olympic medals (Rudolph also won a bronze medal at the 1956 Games in Melbourne) was an inspiration to push myself through to my own finish line.

Motherhood officially arrived September 19, 1960, with the birth of Edward McDonald Ranger, Jr. (7 pounds, 9 ounces) at the original Florence Crittenton Hospital in Detroit. It was the largest maternity hospital in the nation at the time. Ned's mother, Lena, was in poor health; his youngest sister, Gabrielle Beauregard, brought Lena to the hospital to see her baby's new son. At the time, I had no idea of the tremendous joys that would transpire over our next nineteen years in Michigan.

Let me tell you: These were the days to have babies! New mothers enjoyed a full eight days in the hospital—a mini-vacation, with the baby carted off to the nursery each night at 7 p.m. to leave the new mom in solitude for a full twelve hours of glorious and uninterrupted sleep. I would leisurely leaf through a stack of magazines including *McCall's*, *Ladies Home Journal* and *Good Housekeeping*. Thankfully, I would be blessed with all five of my children to have natural childbirths, with no health complications and similar week-long reprieves from the duties of motherhood.

Shady

Once I returned home, there was one downside to having babies in those days: cloth diapers. Rather than just tossing the malodorous land mines created by each of my successive bundles of joy, I had to spend considerable time with the toxic contents. First, I rinsed the diapers in the toilet with a few quick dunks to remove the bulk contents. Then I soaked them in a bucket filled with a chemical concoction likely manufactured for use only in heavy industry and probably later banned by the FDA for its toxicity levels. Then I'd put them in a plastic bag for the diaper service to pick up. Once the clean diapers came back, we would start the entire process again by pinning the soft cloth around a newborn's freshly powdered and squirming bottom, making certain to poke my own finger, and draw my own blood, rather than the baby's.

Cloth-diaper challenges aside, from the first moment I saw Edward, I knew I was going to love being a mom. After my glorious eight-day spa retreat at the hospital, on September 25 Ned drove us home in our red convertible MG with wire-spoke wheels, as I sat in the tiny front seat holding little Edward. As we opened the front door to our house, the phone was ringing. Ned answered only to hear his sister Gabrielle telling him his mother, Lena, had just died. Because she had been so gravely ill, the general consensus was that she had somehow willed herself to stay alive long enough to see her baby's baby. (On a side note, Ned's older sister Gabrielle lived a long life and only passed away in 2019, at age 97.) For Ned and me both, bringing home an infant completely pushed the normal grieving process to the back burner.

In Michigan, the month of September was an idyllic time to bring home a new baby. In Detroit, we went from summer to fall in this single month as the sun dipped lower in the sky with each passing day. The amount of daylight dwindled, and the average daily high and low temperatures dropped about ten degrees each by month's end. By the time my mother came to stay with us, which she did frequently to lavish the baby with all-out grandmotherly love, she was wheeling a heavily bundled Edward around in his buggy that was almost as big as our MG. Make no mistake: My mother was a tremendous help.

She would be gone for hours pushing Edward, logging up to six or more miles a day. As Halloween came and went, Edward was wearing a full snowsuit on those daily walks, which is why he always had a suntanned little face where the wool didn't quite cover.

Soon after we brought our baby home, a new couple moved in across the street: John and Mary Tulloch, who had a twin boy and girl. Over the years we became very close friends with the Tullochs, including traveling together. Dr. Tulloch was an OB/GYN and would deliver our next four children. Who could say what our future might have held, or how each of our houses would have looked, had he instead been an aluminum siding salesman!

MEANWHILE, that young upstart Kennedy, whose campaign announcement had tracked with my own milestone news in January, made a campaign stop in Michigan. On Labor Day 1960, I had the privilege of seeing him riding down Woodward Avenue perched on the back of an open convertible. Yes, in hindsight it was an ominous harbinger of that horrible day three years later: Our young, vibrant soon-to-be president just innocently wheeling around America in open-air vehicles with the breeze in his luxurious hair—he was spectacularly good-looking with his tanned face and gleaming white teeth, like a movie star—and his beautiful bride by his side, both fully exposed to the elements and lurking evil. Two months later he won the election, defeating then-Vice President Richard Nixon. Just 43, Kennedy was the first Catholic and the youngest person to be elected president.

While I stayed home with Edward, Ned was working long and hard hours at the firm. At the outset they'd focused their practice in an area of law where they could most effectively apply their unique skill set, which was medical and hospital malpractice defense and representing design professionals, engineers, accountants, attorneys and insurance agents in professional liability and malpractice cases. Ned normally left each morning around 7:30 a.m. His first step in getting to work was pulling the blanket off the hood of the MG in the carport; it was notoriously difficult to start, especially during the Michigan winter. Once the engine started, he was underway. While the sporty little car was easy to park in the city and conjured images of a beautiful, carefree couple holidaying on the Riviera, this particular vehicle was not ideal as a commuter car in the Arctic winds of the Michigan peninsula. By the time Ned arrived at the Penobscot Building, in downtown Detroit, he could barely unclench his frozen hands from the steering wheel. He followed that routine, eventually from several different houses in greater Detroit, for the next twenty years—until we followed our own Manifest Destiny to a warmer climate in 1979.

Located in downtown Detroit, Sullivan, Sullivan, Ranger & Ward did well from the outset. When Ned was in trial and working long hours, which was frequently, Edward and I would be on our own. The glorious invention I'd seen at the World's Fair with my dad, the television, kept us entertained with fare from the dumb-but-entertaining (*The Beverly Hillbillies*) to the clever (*The Lucy Show*) and, of course, the more cerebral *Perry Mason*, which might have cast the die for little Edward in choosing his future career as a lawyer when he heard the fictional character say, "A toast to the things for which there are no substitutes: Good friends, happy days and... victory." Similarly, Edward's attorney father attended a lot of bar association meetings and business functions while I stayed busy at home with my infant, who was soon a toddler on the run.

When I got pregnant fourteen months after Edward was born, it was a watershed time: Operation Chopper began, as America's first combat mission in the Vietnam War. The devastation, loss of life and full tragedy would be a permanent and painful backdrop to our daily lives for the next dozen years. Stateside, Chubby Checker's "The Twist" dance craze was all the rage, a stunning juxtaposition of innocence to the slow revelation of insanity in Asian jungles. Amid that same daily compartmentalization—the tragic against the mundane—we realized we were going to need a bigger house. We started driving neighborhoods and looking at houses on the east side of Detroit,

"Mothers hold their children's hands for a short while, but their hearts forever."

—Unknown

where four of Ned's six sisters lived. Our friend Dr. Tulloch delivered our second son, Patrick Arthur, on December 15, 1962, at Harper Hospital in Detroit.

By fall 1963, President Kennedy and his political advisers were laying the groundwork for his second presidential campaign. We had no reason to believe he would not be re-elected. As Ned spent more and more time in trials, and I wrangled my two boys at home, Kennedy traveled west in September, to nine different states in less than a week, to highlight his policy positions on protecting natural resources and conservation efforts, education, national security and world peace.

Busy with work and raising our two children, Ned and I couldn't have known that what still appeared to be a calm kettle on the stove was about to boil over. Very quietly, although U.S. government officials denied that the United States even had combat soldiers in South Vietnam, our troops were routinely engaged in combat operations against the Viet Cong. In 1963 alone, 122 of our boys would not come home, and the total number of U.S. soldiers in South Vietnam would surpass 16,000 by year's end. Then, on November 22, 1963, I got a call from my maternal Aunt Honey (Barbara), who was crying and barely able to tell me that President Kennedy had been assassinated in Dallas. We had just arrived home from the Edgewater Beach Hotel in Chicago. There was an instant sea change in our town, throughout Michigan and the country, as a sadness and a pall blanketed the nation. I remember seeing people who were just walking around in shock and crying from the loss. The tumult of the 1960s was officially underway.

After living in our first house several years, in 1963 we moved to 456 Shelbourne Road in Grosse Pointe Farms, which was twenty-one miles east near Lake St. Clair. Although we had leaped to the apex of the perceived class and social hierarchy with an official "Grosse Pointe" address, it didn't really feel that way at the time. Instead, we had found a simple and modest ranch house that you might find anywhere in the Midwest. More important, this was the home where we would bring home our next two children: Julia Ann (November 12, 1964) and Jacqueline Ann (August 13, 1966), who were also both born at

Harper Hospital in Detroit. We were equally thrilled to welcome our first daughter, whom we called Julie, after two sons, and then a second daughter, whom we called Jackie, to fully balance the household.

Jackie's arrival was an event unto itself. In August 1966 Ned took our three children on a vacation to Washington, D.C. Looking back, I'm still not sure why my husband decided to venture off on a two-week vacation while I was left home eight-and-a-half months pregnant; to this day I don't know! Perhaps it was a well-intended gesture to give me some peace and quiet at home to rest. However, when the labor pains came, I was home alone and left to fend for myself. I called a taxi company and tried to stay calm as I explained my condition and the urgency. When the taxi arrived, I waddled out to the curb, climbed in and was soon checking myself into Harper Hospital. Once there, I immediately called all four of Ned's sisters to let them know what was happening. The woman at the front desk first asked why I was there, and I said to have a baby. Once I was checked in and settled in my room, a fire alarm went off.

"Good Lord," I said aloud. "What next?"

The hospital staff evacuated everyone, including rolling me outside in a wheelchair. A few minutes later they wheeled me back inside. Jacqueline Ann was born while her father, two older brothers and older sister braved the August heat and humidity of Washington, D.C. Having Jackie was a defining moment for Ned and me. We went from being a busy couple to a life with four young children in less than six years. Ned and I had quickly, and mostly easily, found our parenting groove when there had just been Edward and Patrick. When Jackie was born, however, there was no way getting around it: The household just exploded.

In a quick span, we went from having one toddler to multiple toddlers and a new baby girl simultaneously. As we brought home each new child, the household got exponentially more hectic, with so many toys scattered you could barely see the floor. Ned and I should have bought stock in Fisher-Price toys, because we seemed to have at least two of everything they manufactured. Of particular help was their

"Parents' Guide" catalog that detailed the cornucopia of "The Finest of Playthings for Preschoolers" or, as a clever copywriter the likes of whom I might have known in my Kenyon & Eckhardt days put it: "Little toys for creepers and toddlers." Toddlers, yes, and depending on the day, "creepers" indeed. Our little creepers, Edward, Patrick and Julie, were always going in three different directions simultaneously. Our baby girl Jackie was, thankfully, not yet mobile. We had so many sets of the "Educational Blocks," which according to our "Parents' Guide" were "beautifully shaped and sanded Ponderosa Pine." While that statement was true, the catalog might have also mentioned that these hefty blocks of hewn pine were also guaranteed to cause severe distress, tears and bruising when thrown by children living in groups of two or more, and/or cause breakage and damage to common household items such as lamps, windows and glassware.

Our invaluable catalog told us, too, that the "fascinating sounds, interesting shapes, exciting actions and colorful figures are carefully combined to aid the preschooler's mental and physical development." Again, what they failed to mention is that there was often an inverse relationship with the very same toy, which is to say that some of the toys would drive the parents into madness. There was no single plaything ever invented, by Fisher-Price or any other toy manufacturer in the history of the United States, that had this twin power to entertain children and drive parents insane more than the now-classic Corn Popper. Our "Parents' Guide" described the toy this way: "Wood balls 'poppity-pop' against acetate dome. Boys and girls 1-3." In some sleep-deprived moment of weakness we bought three of these machines, so Edward, Patrick and Julie would each have their own rather than fighting over who-got-it-when. We never stopped to consider the sheer volume of one of these Corn Poppers in motion, with multiple wooden balls bouncing off hard plastic, let alone three simultaneously. For this toy, the helpful "Parents' Guide" should have added this dire warning: "Caution: Exposure to more than seven minutes of the 'poppity-pop' sound may cause an uncontrollable urge in adults to smash the acetate

dome against a brick wall." That was the soundtrack of our lives—
love, joy and madness—for many years.

What does Julie have in her mouth? Poppity-pop!
Did Edward just put a raisin up his nose? Poppity-pop!
Patrick, did you throw that block at your sister?
Poppity-pop!
Who knocked over the diaper pail (thus creating a toxic
spill of the heavy-industry soaking solution)? Poppity-pop!
Jackie, again? We just changed your diaper two minutes
ago! Poppity-pop!

When dinnertime rolled around, we usually kept it simple: Kraft
macaroni and cheese and sloppy Joes were staples in our household.
And, of course, like many 1960s parents, my primary stop when
food shopping was the supermarket freezer case. In fact, in hindsight
I would have liked to pen a note of gratitude to E. Robert Kinney
for making our years of child-rearing infinitely easier with his simple
invention. It was he who single-handedly ended a million dinner-
table standoffs between moms like me and their children with the
ultimate "healthy" food in disguise: fish sticks. When Kinney was
at Gorton-Pew Fisheries in the 1950s, he transformed mild cod into
a crunchy vehicle for covertly delivering protein in a package my
children eagerly scarfed with their fingers. The key, of course, was
buckets of tartar sauce to further disguise any actual fish taste and
complete the ruse even as my children clamored for more. Welcome
to the 1960s: Poppity-pop, processed fish sticks and a deepening war
crisis halfway around the globe.

Finally, at the end of every long, crazy, fun and exhilarating day,
when I collapsed into my own bed after multiple tuck-ins, water
requests, bathroom visits and a last diaper change, I simply thanked
God for all my blessings. Parenting challenges and all, there was
nothing better than being a mom after growing up an only child.
Having my own large family, poppity-pop and all, was everything to
me. For me, this was as good as it could get.

Shady

ORIGINALLY incorporated in 1927 as the Village of Lochmoor, Grosse Pointe is small in acreage—only covering an area of 3.28 square miles—and also pristine and premiere. One of Detroit's grandest enclaves and its first commuter suburb, the community along Lake St. Clair is full of cottages, resorts, farms and lakefront mansions divided into five different communities: Grosse Pointe Farms (northernmost), Grosse Pointe Park, Grosse Pointe Shores, Grosse Pointe Woods and Grosse Pointe City. A long list of the well-heeled and well-known, past and present, had a Grosse Pointe address. Edsel Ford, the automaker, resided and died in Grosse Pointe Shores. At this writing Edsel Ford II resides in Grosse Pointe Farms. Henry Ford II, auto executive, lived in Grosse Pointe, as does his granddaughter Elena Ford, also an auto executive at the family business who resides in Grosse Pointe Farms. Kirk Gibson, a former baseball player for the hometown Detroit Tigers, makes his home in Grosse Pointe. The American film scion John Hughes, who gave us *Home Alone* and *Ferris Bueller's Day Off* among other movies, grew up in Grosse Pointe. John Cusack starred in a 1997 film that played on the town's subdivisions in its title, *Grosse Pointe Blank*. The roads throughout Grosse Pointe are full of mansions where grand porte-cocheres and service kitchens are as common as plumbing. *The Grosse Pointe News* had a standing "Butlers" heading in its classified advertisement section.

Our home on Shelbourne Road was a modest three-bedroom, two-bath, 1,461-square-foot house built in 1952. It was a ranch style with a nice backyard. It was not ostentatious in any way. The big luxury was that we had a garage for the first time, which would keep our vehicle warm enough to facilitate early morning starts during the ice-bound winter. With a growing brood, we also added a larger family vehicle.

As part of his law firm benefits, we had a membership at the Grosse Pointe Yacht Club, which was one mile from where we lived. In the summer, the children would get in their Sunfish sailboats for races staged by the Yacht Club, and navigate Lake St. Clair. We had access to Ned's company prop plane, and I remember a family trip to New York as we flew over the Statue of Liberty and the bridges connecting Manhattan to the outer boroughs. Before departure, back in the driveway at our house in Grosse Pointe, we had to use a scale to carefully check the weight of each suitcase to ensure we didn't exceed the limit for takeoff. While we were officially part of the Midwest glitterati with our Grosse Pointe address and access to some privileged niceties, we really didn't see ourselves as anything other than normal Midwesterners.

Ned was still the hard-working son of immigrants, one of nine children who started with almost nothing and forged his own way through law school. And I was the daughter who'd lost her own hard-working dad at 6 1/2 years old. While I'd grown up comfortably, we certainly were not rich. Neither Ned nor I had been bred and raised among the silver-spoon set. Nor had we sought that life for ourselves. Instead, we quietly moved into their world and wondered aloud to each other whether we'd ever be fully accepted into the aristocracy. We sometimes encountered the scions of snobbery—those who inquired about our grandparents' surnames to see if we were of proper breeding stock—but we didn't let it affect or change us. While Ned worked, I was at home with our two boys, an energetic toddler hard-wired to find ways to harm herself, and a newborn.

Edward started kindergarten in 1965, which reduced the workload by one during school hours. Nonetheless, I was always on the run changing Jackie's diapers and keeping Julie and Patrick from sticking metal objects into electrical outlets. Four young children meant daily doses of laughter, smiles, tears, frustration and the looming possibly of another trip to the emergency room. We experienced many of those emotions later when Edward, who was by then in fourth grade, dressed up as his namesake Saint Edward for All Saint's Day. Now, when I say "dress up" I don't mean just throwing a sheet over him as a pulpit robe. We got him the pulpit robe, of course, along with a crown, a purple cape with faux fur trim and a scepter. He looked resplendent as I sent him off to the bus stop that morning. Except, as I would learn only when he came home, he was the only kid dressed up that day.

Having four children also meant the probability that every day at least one of the children might not be having their best day. I did my best to keep the house clean, which started each day as a settled snow globe. Once all the feet hit the ground, however, and started shaking it up, I had no chance until they were all back in bed that night. I also felt like a part-time nail technician with forty fingernails and forty toenails to clip (not to mention the endless cuts, scrapes and owies on those eighty digits). Our bedtime routine was a two-hour ritual until the last child was settled, which gave me thirty minutes to put the house back together before starting the routine again the next morning. My mother was such a big help to me in these busy days. I think she truly enjoyed the constant chaos as much as I did, as a new crisis was always looming—such as when a child goes missing.

It was a Sunday, and we were all getting ready for an early dinner with the Pittel family who lived next door. Once I had Edward and Patrick dressed and ready and was holding baby Jackie, I realized I'd briefly lost track of Julie.

"Where's Julie?" I asked Ned.

"I don't know."

We called out to her, and it didn't take long to sweep our small home and realize Julie was nowhere to be seen. We immediately panicked. We only lived one block from Mack Avenue, a busy six-lane thoroughfare equivalent to Scottsdale Road in Arizona. The moment I realized she was not in my view, I was beset with that unmistakable sinking panic every parent knows all too well. We immediately called the Grosse Pointe police station.

Apparently Julie had wandered out of our house, walked down Shelbourne to Mack Avenue in her beautiful white nylon coat and turned right. Some Good Samaritan must have seen our little girl, pulled over, picked her up and drove her to the police station.

"She's sitting on our counter right now," the policeman told me over the phone. A wave of immense relief swept through me as I realized she was safe. In the end, the resolution came as we rushed into the Grosse Pointe police station to see a group of officers fawning over the almost-3-year-old sitting on the front counter in her fancy white coat. Somewhere, at the bottom of a box, I still have the police incident report documenting that horrifying moment I'll never forget.

ONE highlight was our annual summer getaways, each July from 1967 through 1970, when we would rent a lovely cottage at Pointe aux Barques. Located on Lake Huron two and a half hours straight north of Detroit via Interstate 69, Pointe aux Barques was a simple cluster of charming cottages—many of them owned by the prominent automobile families of Detroit—that transported us back to a simpler time. Without a single traffic light or skyscraper, this was a place we could slow down, decompress and turn the children loose along the beach and shaded woodland trails. Ned would end his work week Friday afternoon in downtown Detroit and be in Pointe aux Barques by dinnertime. We'd enjoy the weekend together as a family before Ned returned to downtown Detroit early Monday morning to start his work week. I would spend Monday through Friday keeping tabs on the children and enjoying the clean air and sunshine.

While the children played nearby, I would sit and watch the sailboats, kayaks and water-skiers carving wakes through crystal-blue Alaska Bay. I'd lube us all up with baby oil, in the days before sunscreen, and bring along a picnic basket. There was a nine-hole golf course, tennis courts and a clubhouse, but we spent our time ad hoc, playing and exploring. The family focus of our time there each summer, along with the quiet beauty of the natural setting, imprinted indelible memories I can still vividly recall more than five decades later.

An intertwined memory from that same time, and at the other end of the spectrum of tranquility, hit us squarely on the morning of Monday, July 24, 1967.

As we enjoyed this privileged life, there was a deeper undercurrent in our beloved Detroit, which involved high levels of frustration, resentment and anger in our African-American community. Lack of jobs and opportunities, extreme poverty, racism, segregation and police brutality were a dangerous, simmering concoction ready to explode. While we were asleep in a pristine rented cottage at Pointe aux Barques, police raided an illegal after-hours drinking club on a steamy July night. On the night of the raid, the speakeasy was packed with revelers welcoming home two returning Vietnam War veterans. The police arrested every patron in the place, including eighty-two African Americans. That raid was the spark that ignited the powder keg. Protestors vandalized property, looted businesses and started fires. The action escalated as police officers and protesters clashed. As the violence spread, police lost control of the situation.

Cloistered in our Pointe aux Barques bubble—and long before the days of 24/7 cable news, smart phones and social media—we hadn't heard anything about what was happening in Detroit. Ned left as planned on Monday morning and headed south to Detroit, driving through a cool mist. It was while he was in the car listening to the radio that he heard the warnings about the riots and burning in Detroit. There was a public advisory for all citizens to avoid the vicinity. Ned found an off-ramp and made a U-turn back to Pointe aux Barques. To quell the chaos, the Michigan governor deployed more than 9,000 members of the U.S. National Guard, along with 800 state police officers. President Johnson also dispatched U.S. Army troops to the maelstrom. While the militarized response tamped down the immediate threat, the reality of police brutality and racial profiling on Detroit's streets would continue unchecked. It saddened Ned and me alike, that there was this devastating split between the economic ruling class and an African-American underclass forced into substandard housing. For us, the riots—with the death toll, injuries and huge property damage—were merely chilling reminders of much deeper societal fissures we felt powerless to change.

ECONOMIC disparity and larger societal issues aside, our immediate reality was that with a family that had grown to four children, we were very cramped in our small ranch house. To alleviate that, in 1968 we moved a short distance to a larger, two-story Spanish-style house at 335 Grosse Pointe Boulevard, also in Grosse Pointe Farms, near Moross Road and one block from Lake St. Clair.

Our house at 335 Grosse Pointe Boulevard.

Our first four children all attended Kerby Elementary in Grosse Pointe Farms, and then Edward, Patrick and Julie went on to Grosse Pointe South High School. Edward would graduate from high school in 1978, while Julie would only attend there for one year because of our eventual move west. I signed up as Room Mother for all my children, and went on every field trip with each of the eventual five children. We always invited the home room teachers to our house for an end-of-school luncheon. Our children's schedules were jammed with baseball, tennis, soccer, ballet, gymnastics, piano lessons and Junior Assembly dances.

Shady

In 1968 we embraced our Americana lifestyle and purchased a true family automobile. Ned splurged on our first new car, and it was the cream of the crop for that model year: a Ford Country Squire Limited. Yellow with fake wood paneling, the eight-cylinder beast sported AM radio and tinted glass. Ned paid $3,935.48 out the door that day in May, to the dealership of Roy O'Brien on 9 Mile Road in St. Clair Shores. We also had a small Boston Whaler for fishing, and a thirty-two-foot Chris-Craft cruiser; we kept them both at the pier. We lived only one block from Lake St. Clair, and the water was a regular part of our routine starting in April, when we could finally start shedding the winter layers. Each of the five Grosse Pointe municipalities had its own designated pier. We used our Boston Whaler for tooling around, water skiing and fishing. For longer journeys, we took the Chris-Craft. Springtime meant our annual family trip to Florida or Hilton Head Island in South Carolina, by commercial airline. As we left the lingering gray cold, our only prayer was for sunshine upon our arrival.

By May we took regular walks to the pier and had family picnics. When summer arrived, we took the boat to Harsens Island, about forty-five minutes away across the water, to spend a weekend. Two of our favorite places to eat there were Brown's Bar and San Souci Bar. If the smelt were running, we'd continue north to Algonac and Henry's Restaurant to feast on that sublime Midwestern fare. We also took trips to the Upper Peninsula, where we stayed on Mackinac Island in the Grand Hotel. Michigan summers on the water also meant doing battle with the ubiquitous and primary predators, which were mosquitoes the size of cherry tomatoes.

As summer faded and the leaves started to turn in October, fall was another beautiful time in Michigan. Two or three times before the big snows came, we'd pile into the car and drive to Franklin Cider Mill in Franklin. The six of us would drink hot cider and eat hot corn on the cob straight out of the kettle and slathered with butter, as well as hot cinnamon doughnuts. Apparently not yet aware that carb-overload and cholesterol levels were a real thing, from there we'd go to the

Country Inn restaurant, owned by Pepe, for barbecue ribs. On the way home, we listened to John Denver's "Country Roads" and Jim Croce singing "Bad, Bad Leroy Brown."

When the snow arrived, we drove three-and-a-half hours each way to the Otsego Ski Club in Gaylord, Michigan, where we were members. Snow permitting, we did a lot of skiing in January, February and March. If mosquitoes were our summer nemesis, then the winter opponent was the bitter-cold, miserable weather. It was almost guaranteed, like Swiss trains arriving on time, that the power would go out at home at least once during January or February. That meant it was an annual affair when Ned and I piled everyone into the Country Squire and spent a couple nights at the Weber Inn in Ann Arbor, which had one of the few indoor, heated swimming pools in Michigan open to the public. Fast-forward forty years, to 2014, and I would return with my daughter Julie and her family for the graduation of my oldest grandson, Tommy Adelson, from the University of Michigan. Some things never change, like the Weber Inn, which was just as it had been forty years prior, with all the locals singing in the bar, which was bittersweet.

As our children hit their early teen years, they were introduced to Junior Assembly at the Grosse Pointe Country Club, where they would learn social conduct through ballroom dance. With the goal of trying to help children develop in mind, body and spirit, Junior Assembly was an organization started in 1940 by Pearl C. Porter and a group of mothers to give children more confidence and poise through social conduct—i.e., throw a bunch of children together at a ballroom dance and see what happens. Ned and I found a window where we could peek in and watch as our children interacted with others in these early social lessons. I like to believe it gave our children a little more confidence, or maybe the forced social interaction just made them anxious.

That's all to say that finally, in early 1972, Ned and I planned an evening out as a couple, which would be the first time we'd leave the four children home alone: Edward, 12; Patrick, 10; Julie, 8; and Jackie, 6. We sat them all down before leaving, with a somber briefing that might have surpassed the planning for the Apollo 16 mission launched that year. After laying out all the ground rules and writing down the name of where we would be—Joe Muer Seafood—along with the phone number, Ned and I climbed in our yellow Country Squire and slipped into the Midwestern night.

What could go wrong, right?

The restaurant was packed that night, but we didn't mind: Any time we had to wait was more couple time together. While we were waiting at the bar for our table, suddenly over the loudspeaker I heard, "Phone call for Sandy Ranger."

I went to the house phone, said "Hello" and a male voice said, "This is Sergeant Smith of the Grosse Pointe Farms Police Department. I'm at your house with your four children."

My first thought: Not good! "Please tell me what's going on!"

He said, "Edward told me that Julie opened the freezer door and went to get some ice cubes. Unfortunately, her hands were damp and ice cubes stuck to all ten fingers. Edward said, 'No problem, Julie, I can help you.' He pulled them each off aggressively, and all ten fingers started bleeding profusely. He gave her a towel, panicked and then decided he'd better call the police department."

So much for our first night out, which had lasted all of forty-five minutes. "I'm so sorry, Sergeant Smith. We're on our way."

BY May 1972 I was feeling very sick, and had been for some time. I made a doctor appointment, thinking I needed an antibiotic. After I saw the doctor, he informed me that I could look forward to feeling better in about six-and-a-half months, after delivering my fifth child. Needless to say, I left that examination room in a state of shock. Indeed, that was an eventful year for us. On October 26, my mom, 77, died at St. John's Hospital. She had moved in with us in late 1965, on Grosse Pointe Boulevard, and had been a tremendous help with the children. The official cause of death was myocardial infarction—a heart attack.

Snady

We went from that sadness to joyful elation in December. Similar to what I had gone through with Jackie, I was again eight-and-a-half months pregnant when the family decided to venture to Sun Valley, Idaho, to go skiing, leaving me to once again fend for myself in my plump condition. When the labor pains came I was again home alone, and again called for a taxi, which took me to St. John's Hospital only about a mile away. Peter Fall was born in 1972 on my mother's birthday, December 18, six weeks after she had died. When they heard the big news, my family came home. A week later, Ned and I took Peter home on Christmas Day in a Santa Claus onesie and red hat. The nurses put all the babies going home on Christmas day in a big red stocking. Of course, there were no child seats in those days. Ned drove, and I held my new baby in his Christmas stocking. When we arrived home all four children had noses pressed against the dining room window looking out, not so much anxious to see their new baby brother but more anxiously counting down the seconds to opening their Christmas presents under the tree.

Once I was feeling better and back on my feet, one of my first projects was redecorating Julie and Jackie's bedroom. For some reason I was fixated on finding two antique spindle beds, which I thought would be the crowning touch of my designer efforts. I placed a small classified advertisement in the Grosse Pointe News. My advertisement generated exactly one response, a phone call from a genial woman in Grosse Pointe Park. I made arrangements to borrow a van and go to her house, because she indeed had two yellow spindle beds hand-painted with green leaves. It turned out she was Mrs. Mary Wilson, spouse of Ralph Wilson, founder and owner of the Buffalo Bills National Football League team. As I chatted with Mrs. Wilson she asked whether, as a young bride, I might need some nice china and crystal.

"Not really," I said.

"Well," she said. "I don't know what to do with them." She led me to a large collection of beautiful white china trimmed in gold, along with elegant crystal glasses. She'd already made up her mind when she

82

filled three boxes with china and crystal and said, "You enjoy these, honey. Every young person should have a good set of dishes and crystal."

Peter and me.

NOW a family of seven, in August 1974, we took our boat to Put-In-Bay, Ohio, a village on Lake Erie, to spend two nights. As we skimmed across the water, the sky quickly darkened, and Ned and I watched in horror as jagged lightning stabbed the horizon. We found the Wyandotte Yacht Club for shelter, pulled into an open slip and settled in for the storm to pass. Ned flipped on our little black-and-white TV on the boat, and we all watched President Nixon climbing the stairs on the helicopter and waving goodbye for the last time.

The next summer, on a sticky July day, Ned and I had lunch at the Machus Red Fox restaurant in Bloomfield Township. We went there occasionally because they had good food and, notably, it was quite the hangout where you might see a politician, high-profile local celebrity or other notables. The next day, on July 30, 1975, Jimmy Hoffa strode

Julie (L), me and Jackie at the Grosse Pointe "Lawyers' Wives Fashion Show."

into the same restaurant, had lunch and was never seen again, with no clues as to what happened to him. He was last seen in the parking lot of "our" restaurant in Bloomfield Township.

When our fifth child, Peter, was 4 years old, in 1976, he attended the only Montessori school in Grosse Pointe Farms. One of his classmates, Eddie Patton, invited Peter to his birthday party. When I heard about this I was way more excited than Peter, because I knew Eddie's mother was Gladys Knight, and his father had been a Pip. Eddie Patton's party was, of course, not going to be pin-the-tail-on-the-donkey and Kool-Aid in a backyard, but rather was being held at one of the fanciest stops in Detroit, the Book-Cadillac Hotel. For a Detroit transplant such as myself and a true Motown fan, I believed this event would be a crowning moment. I began my preparations as though I'd been invited to the Oscars. Ned, too, was excited that we were going to rub shoulders with music immortality.

On the appointed day all three of us got dressed to the nines and climbed inside the Country Squire for the twenty-minute drive downtown. When we arrived, we took the elevator to the room number we'd been given, where a thickset man in a suit stood with his arms crossed. We smiled and braced ourselves for the moment.

"This is Peter Ranger," we said proudly, as though he were in the band himself and ready to take his spot behind the drum set. "We are his parents."

The bodyguard did not embrace us as though we were part of the inner circle. Instead, he opened the door and held his arm against the jamb, creating a child-size opening for Peter.

"Go ahead, Peter," he said, smiling. Our son crossed the metaphorical velvet rope and left us tippy-toed and peering for any glimpse of celebrity before the door slammed shut.

"Thank you," the bodyguard said. "If you would be good enough to pick up Peter at this same spot in two-and-a-half hours, that would be wonderful."

We both tried to play it off, but if the bodyguard hadn't read any disappointment on my face, surely he was wondering why I was in such formal dress on a Saturday afternoon. My takeaway that day: Always keep your expectations low, and you will never be disappointed. Collectively, through the first forty years of my life—and motherhood especially—I had developed some key traits: Keep a positive attitude, enjoy what you're doing (see: toxic diapers) and develop and lean on a sense of humor.

Poppity-pop!

Part II

MOVING

– Chapter 5 –

GO WEST, DAD

ALTHOUGH WE DID NOT GLIMPSE GLADYS KNIGHT nor any Pip in 1976, we did celebrate the Bicentennial of our nation. As a legal practitioner, Ned was especially proud of our relatively young nation and democratic experiment, with fully one-third of our government, the judicial branch, grounded in the rule of law. The U.S. Bicentennial sparked widespread interest in American history, with museums and historical sites across the country rolling out programs and celebrations marking two hundred years of shared history. In greater Detroit, that history was inextricably linked to the birth of the automobile. Curators at two of our local museums, Greenfield Village and Henry Ford Museum, launched an impressive schedule of Bicentennial events, activities and exhibits that drew record crowds in 1976, including our brood of five.

In January of the next year, Jimmy Carter took his oath as thirty-ninth president of the United States of America. Ned and I were relieved, mostly, as the leadership change finally closed the chapter on the Vietnam-Nixon-Gerald Ford era. When Carter pardoned Vietnam War draft evaders, the benevolent act was one of the first steps in addressing the troubling reality of the first failed U.S. military campaign. Later that month, on January 23, 130 million other Americans and I started watching *Roots*, which aired on ABC for eight consecutive nights. My sons Edward and Patrick remember watching with me. In fact, people in eighty-five percent of all television homes saw all or part of the miniseries, a feat I doubt we'll ever repeat with our far-flung entertainment options and streaming services today.

That same month the first personal computer, called the Commodore PET, debuted at the Consumer Electronics Show in Chicago. While I had strolled hand-in-hand with my father through the RCA Pavilion to see those flickering boxes at the dawn of television, almost forty years later I didn't hear anything about the coming age of home and personal technology.

In June 1977, we finally took the children to see *Star Wars* at the Punch and Judy Theatre on Kercheval Avenue in Grosse Pointe Farms, after all the buzz this odd little science fiction story was getting. It was the same month Elvis Presley performed his final concert in Indianapolis; he would be dead two months later. Life rolled on and, in late January 1978, the Great Lakes Blizzard struck the region. Michigan Governor William Milliken declared a state of emergency and marshalled the Michigan National Guard to aid stranded motorists and road crews. Michigan State Police told people to stay away from Traverse City, which got dumped on with two feet of snow. Dubbed one of the worst blizzards in U.S. history, the storm caused tens of millions in damage and killed more than seventy people. In Detroit, we got about eight inches of snow, which for us was a light dusting that barely impacted our daily life. Ned still made it to work, and I sent all the children off to school in their nineteen layers of wool and black boots with the metal clasps.

That spring, Ned and I traveled west of the Mississippi River for the first time, to Arizona on a business trip. Ned was working on a case representing his client Greyhound Corporation, which had its headquarters in Phoenix. Just the two of us took the trip while Ned's sister stayed with our children. While Ned spent his days meeting in windowless offices and poring over documents, I had time to get outside to explore this strange new land. Compared to the verdant countryside of Pennsylvania and Michigan where I'd spent my entire life, the Sonoran Desert was like an oddly beautiful moonscape, and unlike anything I'd ever seen. I'd read my Fodor's guide on the airplane and had prepared myself to be stepping over rattlesnakes and around cacti from the moment we stepped off the jetway. But those tourist clichés were barely part of the complicated entirety called the Sonoran Desert. And I immediately noticed the most fascinating element, the DNA that gives the desert its special character: the subtle and mysterious quality of light that painted the skies a luxurious shade of blue. The skies over metropolitan Phoenix are such a uniquely deep blue, I learned, because the desert air is almost devoid of particles and droplets called aerosols, which can dim the "blueness" we perceive. Apparently, I had lived the first forty-plus years of my life under skies diluted with white light. It wasn't until I arrived in Arizona that I saw a truly blue sky, a color so rich and radiant I could not stop staring upward. I was equally enthralled by another unique desert phenomenon when I saw a towering dust devil slowly parading across the pool deck at our hotel. This miniature tornado I witnessed was a thermal, a whirlwind created when the heated desert air spirals inward and upward. Ned and I had discovered a sun-splashed new place that, in March, thawed our Midwest bones with daytime highs in the 80s.

Throughout the next year, Ned and I talked about how much we had enjoyed Arizona. Our son Edward was prescient when he said, "Ya' gotta go west, Dad." Indeed, at some point, we started seriously discussing the possibility of moving west. In 1979, Ned had to take another trip to Phoenix, again on behalf of Greyhound Corporation. I was buoyed by the news and tried to explain to my children just how blue the April sky would be over Arizona. This time, we took Julie,

Peter, 7   *Jackie, 13*   *Patrick, 17*

Julie, 15   *Edward, 19*

Jackie and Peter, stayed at McCormick Inn and left our two oldest boys, Edward, 19, and Patrick, 17, home alone. (In hindsight, this was not our best strategic move as parents, and the exact details of what transpired in our absence may never be fully known. One piece of evidence that could not be explained away was our nearly totaled Ford Mustang, and Ned wanted to ground both boys for the remainder of their natural-born lives, into adulthood and beyond.) This second trip immediately reaffirmed what had started a year earlier: We were both smitten with Arizona. "My" radiant blue sky was there to greet me once again, except this time as I tried to convey the joy to my children they mostly looked at me like I was crazy.

Toward the end of our visit we saw a sign along Lincoln Road in Paradise Valley and, on a whim, went to an open house for a new residential development called Finisterre, which means "Land's End." The development comprised an entire city block and was bordered by Lincoln Drive to the north and E. McDonald Road to the south, which we immediately believed was a good omen because Ned's name was "Edward McDonald," making "E. McDonald Road" very apropos.

It was just a few days before Easter 1979. If moving west was to be, then this was our own Manifest Destiny: Land's End, the farthest point of our migration. Before we finished walking through the model home, Ned and I were formulating our offer. We put the figure in writing and waited. It was on our return trip to Detroit, during a stopover in Denver, that Ned retrieved a voicemail message: They had accepted our offer for the home at 6221 E. Naumann Drive in Paradise Valley. We were the eighth family to buy there, in a gated subdivision at 61st Street and Lincoln Road that would eventually include more than ninety custom homes. Our official close of escrow on the property was in late May 1979.

As we started preparing for our move, Ned flipped through his Rolodex (a term my grandchildren will have to search online) for contacts in the Wild West. One of the business cards he came across in that enormous, pre-digital spinning wheel was for Jim Tilker, an attorney in Cheyenne, Wyoming, with whom Ned had worked on a national lawsuit. Synchronously, Jim Tilker told Ned during their phone call that he and his family had recently moved to Scottsdale, and that he was setting up a new law practice in the same town, which was rooted back to 1888 when U.S. Army Chaplain Winfield Scott visited the Salt River Valley and bought 640 acres to start a farming operation.

As Ned talked to his client at Greyhound Corporation about the impending move, the client warned Ned about the impending firestorm known as the desert summer. That is, he told Ned, it would not be a good idea to let our newly purchased house sit unoccupied, devoid of air-conditioning, as the heat of the summer could ravage the property. So Ned approached our oldest son Edward and, despite the still-sensitive issue with the Mustang, asked him to act as our advance scout. The plan was for Edward to head west in a rented U-Haul truck with a few of our prized possessions, some of his clothes and personal belongings, and a bed so he could set up in our new house. Edward had just completed his first year at Oakland University in southeast Michigan. It wasn't difficult for him to convince a good friend of his to drive out with him, enjoy a few days in the sun and then return to Michigan on a flight Ned would cover as part of the plan. Edward arrived in the desert in June and quickly found two part-time jobs as a lifeguard: at the Arizona Biltmore hotel in Phoenix, where he'd be poolside in the mornings, and at Camelback Inn Resort in Paradise Valley in the afternoons. Edward, a good-looking 19-year-old, loved his solo time in the desert, poolside by day and living in our 4,500-square-foot house, to which we later added 1,500 square feet, including a full guest house. (In hindsight, that might not have been a good idea, because all our out-of-town visitors knew they had a place to stay.)

Over the summer our sense of excitement and anticipation built steadily. Ned had a law practice to close out, and I had a household to get packed and shipped across the country. Finally, in August 1979 I stood in the driveway with Patrick, Jackie, Julie and Peter as we watched the truck drive away with the bulk of our belongings. The next day, on Sunday, we piled into two cars to caravan across America. I was in a dark gray Chevy Blazer, with Ned's sister Isabel; Jackie, 13; and Julie, 14, who would cry through all 2,000 miles as she faced the grim reality of leaving behind her boyfriend. In the other vehicle, our orange Cadillac convertible the length of a city block, were Ned; Patrick, 16; and Peter, 6.

With our three teenagers loaded—and a fourth prowling a western city all on his own—and our youngest prepped with toys, games and snacks, I followed Ned onto Grosse Pointe Boulevard as our journey began. We were at the end of a decade, the 1970s, which had been wonderful, fun-filled years for us, with more laughter than I could have ever dreamed. There were tears and challenges, too, but we were choosing to leave behind the place where Ned and I had met and had started our respective careers and our family. We had carved out a good life, finding our way among the silver-spoon set, and made the most of it all even in the grips of the harsh winters. Why then were we leaving this place that had worked so well for us? Would we regret this move; i.e., were we selling our stock too soon, one that was poised to double and triple again? It's odd, but as we drove past the diorama of our Midwestern life—the well-tended lawns at the summer peak of green thickness, the children' schools, the park and the sidewalk we'd traveled hundreds of times as a family down to Lake St. Clair—I never once questioned the move or doubted it was the right thing to do. We were closing a chapter that marked the end of a decade and a wonderful time in a wonderful place. And I somehow knew the next chapter—2,000 miles of interstate concrete west from that point—was going to be even better.

After fiddling with the radio for several miles, Jackie finally settled on an incomprehensible song, "Blinded by the Light," a Bruce Springsteen cover from Manfred Mann's Earth Band. I had no idea what they were singing, but with the windows down and the smell of a warm Michigan summer day swirling around the interior of the Blazer, the upbeat energy of the song carried us into our adventure. We were all, indeed, *revved up like a deuce/another runner in the night.*

"Washington is not a place to live in. The rents are high, the food is bad, the dust is disgusting and the morals are deplorable. Go West, young man, go West and grow up with the country."

—Horace Greeley

Shady

Ned had carefully mapped out our journey, which would take us about thirty hours of drive time. When he added in a couple of hours each day for restroom breaks and a lunch stop, we'd be on the road for four long days. We headed southwest, soon left Michigan, cut through the northwest corner of Ohio and into endless miles of verdant Indiana farmland. We passed through Indianapolis before noon and eventually into Illinois. As we rolled into St. Louis by dinnertime, the stainless-steel Gateway Arch came into view; it was the world's tallest arch at 630 feet, and had only been completed in 1965. This was an apropos marker for this journey, our own "Gateway to the West" perched at the site of St. Louis's founding on the west bank of the Mississippi River.

Day Two was a long one, because Ned wanted to take a big bite of mileage: St. Louis to Amarillo, Texas, which was eleven hours away. As we started rolling west again it was still dark. With my two teenage girls Julie and Jackie already asleep in the backseat (when Julie wasn't sleeping she was crying, pining for the boyfriend she had to leave behind), Isabel and I watched the sunrise illuminate the lush Missouri countryside with green rolling hills, fresh-cut fields and black cows lazily swinging their tails. The coming day and wet smell of cut grass transported me immediately: It could have easily been that I was riding with my dad in Germantown, Pennsylvania, as we drove in the early morning light toward the airplane that awaited us in the hangar. Now, I was on another great adventure, of a different kind, with just as much excitement and wonderment as I had felt as a 5-year-old. Of course I was earthbound, but I was also now the pilot of my own craft. I looked in the rearview mirror at my two sleeping daughters and felt a surge of gratitude, to have five healthy children who—other than Peter, who was still only 6—would soon each leave home to undertake their own adventures. My time with them all at home, amazingly, was fast-running sand through the hourglass now. It seemed we had just been living the poppity-pop chaos of the Corn Popper, the diapers and all the rest. Knowing the fleeting nature of time, I would treasure these next years together as a family in our chosen new home state.

It wasn't until we passed into Oklahoma that the true gravity of our migration hit me squarely. Gone was the greenery and foliage of my youth, replaced by a flat and dusty table-scape stretching in every direction. The stark dryness of these arid lands only intensified when we cut across the panhandle of Texas and into Amarillo. While we had done as Ned desired, taken a big bite of mileage out of our journey, the long day in the car had taken its toll. Jackie was tired, and Julie's eyes were red and puffy from mourning the loss of her boyfriend. I was concerned that she might never stop crying. The boys, Patrick and Peter, were stir-crazy from being in the car so long. Ned, Isabel and I, too, were ready for a quick meal and a good night's sleep. The closest restaurant to our motel was a diner called Country Cookin'. The people who worked there lavished us with warm Texas hospitality, which we appreciated because the Country Cookin' was passable at best. But we really didn't care, because mostly we all just wanted to get back to the motel, pile into our beds and dream of our Manifest Destiny the next day.

On our last day, we drove Interstate 40 west, across New Mexico and into our new home state of Arizona. At Flagstaff, we headed south on Interstate 17. As we dropped in elevation into the lower desert on the outskirts of Phoenix, the sun dropped too, touching the horizon and casting the towering saguaros in a beautiful pink, orange and purple twilight. Even with the sun fading, the temperature was well over one hundred degrees, and beyond anything we'd experienced even on the hottest summer day in Michigan. Windows up and air conditioning blasting, I followed the taillights of the orange Cadillac convertible through the urban labyrinth. Finally, a collective excitement started to grow within the Blazer as we knew we were just ten or so minutes from arriving. Then our headlights illuminated a very large sign: "Welcome to the Town of Paradise Valley." Isabel, Jackie, Julie and I all had goosebumps. Then we noticed something odd: Why was it so dark? The only ambient light was from above, starlight and a glowing moon highlighting the craggy outline of the mountains surrounding us. Julie and Jackie solved the mystery: The town of Paradise Valley had no streetlights. It was eerie and beautiful at the same time. We never forgot this special feeling we all shared on the night of August 21, 1979, and continue to think of it. It didn't take long before we got used to this nightly phenomenon and, eventually, actually found the darkness soothing.

We found our house and parked. Our timing was perfect: Earlier that day the moving truck had arrived and, making his best guesses, Edward directed the movers where to put the furniture and boxes. As we all climbed from the two vehicles, the children scattered in every direction to explore. Julie, as it turned out, had cried so much she blocked her tear ducts. Edward walked out, and as he got closer I could see he was tan, fit and healthy from his lifeguard duties.

Ned and I stood side by side, each with an arm around the other, and looked skyward into the dark stillness of a city suburb with no streetlights. The twinkling starlit night was spectacularly different from the sky we had left behind. From that very moment of planting our family flag in Arizona, we never looked back or regretted our decision to move west and settle in a new place.

And more than forty years later, I still feel the same way: Arizona is my home and will be the final chapter and resting place of my earthbound journey.

— Chapter Six —

ARIZONA DREAMING

THE SAME YEAR WE MADE OUR WESTWARD MIGRATION, the previously exiled Ayatollah Ruhollah Khomeini returned to Tehran, Iran. He replaced Shah Mohammad Reza Pahlavi, who had been in power since 1941, and installed a new government. The Shah had attempted to modernize Iran and Westernize the country in the 1960s. Khomeini expelled all foreigners from Iran, including more than 1,000 U.S. State Department workers. In our corner of the world, we weren't closely following the geopolitics of Iran and this shift to extreme isolationism and shunning Westernization. Those events, however, were the backdrop to a national crisis that would begin just months after our arrival in Arizona.

As the household stirred on our first morning, Ned and I realized just how much we had to do. All the children would start school four days later. With that in mind, we had researched in advance to determine which schools everyone would be attending. From youngest to oldest: Peter and Jackie would be attending Kiva Elementary School on McDonald Drive in Paradise Valley, part of a Scottsdale school district with a wonderful reputation; Peter would start second grade while Jackie would start eighth grade.

For our two high schoolers, Patrick (junior) and Julie (sophomore), we had been drawn to two private Roman Catholic schools adjacent to each other in Phoenix: Xavier College Preparatory and Brophy College Preparatory. Brophy had started in 1928 and, in 1943, the Saint Francis Xavier Parish founded his namesake school. We liked that the twin schools followed a traditional college preparatory curriculum, including an emphasis in English, mathematics, social studies, laboratory sciences, world languages and fine arts. In addition, there were numerous honors and advanced-placement courses available. Although each school was officially single-gender, students at Xavier (staffed by the Sisters of Charity) and Brophy shared classes.

For our oldest, Edward, we looked south to Tucson and the University of Arizona, where he had been accepted and would enroll as a sophomore. He had already completed one year at Oakland University in Michigan. Education-wise, I must say it was an easy adjustment for all five children, and it did not take long before they had each made friends with many of their classmates, many of whom were also transplanted from other states. When everyone we met seemed to be from somewhere else, too, it took away any potential roadblocks as the only newcomers.

Because Julie and Jackie were very involved in tennis, we had researched junior clubs and found one nearby called the Chaparral Racquet Club, within Embassy Suites at the corner of Scottsdale and Chaparral roads. At the helm of the program were a pair of brothers. William "Billy" Lenoir was a three-time All-America (1962-64) at the University of Arizona and an eventual member of the Intercollegiate Tennis Association Hall of Fame. He, along with his brother Carter Lenoir, started training Julie and Jackie once we'd signed them up that first day in town. Likewise, Ned and I played a lot of tennis and found a perfect club at the Registry Resort on Scottsdale Road near Indian

Bend Road. We joined that same day as well. Playing tennis with other couples, as it turned out, was a great way to network and for Ned to make connections for his law practice.

At home, we tackled the stacks of boxes. Before leaving Michigan, we had already gotten rid of a lot of our furniture that we knew would look out of place once transported to the Southwest. Even so, as we started to unpack the boxes and look at some of the furniture we had brought along, in the illuminating new desert light we realized those pieces, too, seemed totally out of place. "Buy new furniture" went on the to-do list for later when we went full-bore in embracing the Southwest look. Because there was so much to do in getting our new house in order, we asked Ned's sister Isabel, who had made the pilgrimage with us from Michigan, if she would like to stay for the next nine months. She was delighted because it meant she, too, could miss the brutal Michigan winter.

We were also looking around for the closest grocery stores, pharmacies, shopping centers and restaurants, including The Magic Pan Creperie. From that day we arrived we were all fascinated and excited to be in Arizona, and felt we were truly in paradise, which we actually were: Paradise Valley. Looking at a map, we realized we could drive two and half hours north and ski in Flagstaff in the winter. From there, another hour or so farther and we'd be at the Grand Canyon. If we drove west from our home we could be in San Diego in less than six hours. To the south, we could drive to Tucson in an hour and a half and, one hour farther, we would be in Mexico. In every direction we saw exciting adventures awaiting us. We started taking weekend trips, with the first to beautiful red-rock Sedona where we spent the day. We couldn't believe the transcendent beauty of Sedona, unlike anything in the Midwest, and we were overwhelmed. We took another trip to Flagstaff and, on a separate weekend, went to the Grand Canyon. This was unbelievable as well, from the greenery of Michigan to this stunningly beautiful landscape carved by the steady work of water over millions of years. We also became very familiar with Tucson through frequent visits to see Edward at the University of Arizona.

We quickly settled in without any major speed bumps, and embraced all the change. Truly, we never looked back. Our new environment was such a stark difference, from the greenery to the unique shades of the desert, but we never pined for Midwest things. We never doubted we had done the right thing.

It didn't take long for all of us to get into the groove of a new routine. It was exciting to have a swimming pool in our backyard that got a lot of use. For Thanksgiving, we were amazed that we could eat outside under our covered patio while all our Michigan friends were starting to complain about the weather. The same was true for Christmas. There was only one looming hurdle with our move: Ned would have to take the Arizona Bar exam. Ned's first opportunity to sit for the exam would be in February 1980. With so many variances in laws from state to state, even as we settled in, Ned began studying. He figured the test would be as demanding as the first time around in Michigan.

As the new decade began, with the Rubik's Cube debuting at the British Toy and Hobby Fair in London, we were fully settled in and smitten with the beautiful desert and cacti. As the brutal Michigan winter socked in our Midwest friends, we started getting calls from them asking whether they could come see us for a few days. We enthusiastically said "Yes!" and became adept as tour guides revealing our strange and wonderful new world.

In the same month that the United States men's Olympic hockey team defeated the Soviet Union in the semifinals in the "Miracle on Ice," Ned took the two-day Arizona Bar exam in February 1980, passed and was admitted. The next day, Ned was reading the *Arizona Republic* newspaper and noticed a classified advertisement placed by a person looking for a partner to share the cost of an airplane. Ned had earned his pilot's license while living in the Midwest, where he logged a lot of hours above Michigan in his firm's company plane. However, the weather often dictated when and how often Ned could take to the skies. He called the listed contact, who was an OB/GYN doctor whose backyard coincidentally abutted ours. Ned and I drove to Scottsdale Airport to see the six-passenger Piper Turbo Lance. After inspecting the plane, talking at length with the owner and discussing the fine details of the financial arrangement, Ned and his new partner shook hands on the spot: It was a done deal. Ned and I now had a half-share in an airplane.

Compared to Michigan, Arizona afforded us an altogether different aviation story, with an average of three-hundred-plus sunny days a year. Imagine the heart-thumping thrill of flying down into, and around, the spectacular Grand Canyon (a practice that is no longer allowed) and then heading south to the Sedona Airport, located high on a butte overlooking that uniquely red landscape. These airborne jaunts, which conjured my youth above the verdant Pennsylvania fields with my father, continued through most of the 1980s, generally in the picture-perfect months of January through May when guests would visit to enjoy the desert and its surroundings at their finest.

THAT first year, we were all so busy with our routines that when May rolled around it was hard to believe the children had already completed one year of schooling in a new state. In June, coinciding with the launch of the first twenty-four hour news channel, Cable News Network (CNN), we went tubing down the Salt River for the first time, which was an experience. It was just so new to us, hundreds of people bobbing around on inner tubes. Floating on the water for hours, in 112-degree heat, sapped all our energy. At one point I fell out of my inner tube and had to cling to a tree. This was a true Arizona experience, one we did together as a family each summer for a few years.

Our first summer in Arizona, we took a road trip to Disneyland and in July went to La Jolla, California, where Julie and Jackie went to a two-week tennis camp at La Jolla Beach and Tennis Club. For all of us in the Ranger clan, 1980 flew by as we settled into our routines. Ned was working hard at the law firm, and I was busy with five children. In November Ronald Reagan defeated Jimmy Carter to become the fortieth president of the United States. The Iran hostage crisis negotiations finally led to the release of the fifty-two American hostages in January 1981. In May, Patrick graduated from Brophy High School and joined his older brother Edward at University of Arizona in late August.

In May 1982, Julie graduated from Xavier High School, and Edward graduated from the University of Arizona with a bachelor's degree in English and Spanish. Julie followed her older brothers to University of Arizona.

In 1983, Edward began studying at Thunderbird School of Global Management in Glendale, in the Masters of Global Management (MIM) program. In 1984, Edward began his studies at ASU College

*"May your neighbors respect you,
trouble neglect you, angels protect you
and heaven accept you."*

—Irish saying

of Law in Tempe. Law school! In 1987 he graduated from both Thunderbird and ASU. It seemed I had just been chasing him as a toddler around the house on Shelbourne Road in Gross Pointe Farms. Now my oldest child was following his father's template with a career in law.

These educational milestones were big markers for me, as this was a time of transition. Through it all, from having our first child to all five, I loved being a mom. In fact, I had loved every minute of it from the time each of our children was born. OK, I was never much of a cook, and had somehow missed the pork-chop wizardry my own mother had demonstrated with such ease. Then again, none of my children ever went hungry. It was odd, then, that during that time period of raising, Ned and I and most of our friends had frequent dinner parties. It was remarkable how I could flip a switch and, all by myself, turn out a delectable beef tenderloin dinner with all the trimmings. I was like two different people: fish sticks for the children during the week and, on Saturday night, I morphed into Julia Child. I would pit my soups, split pea and navy bean, against anyone; I used a wonderful honey-glazed ham as the base.

Culinary skills aside, in every other motherhood capacity I was at my best when engaged with my children. Throughout their schooling, I think I went on just about every field trip with each child. I fixed boo-boos, packed lunches and soothed hurt feelings. I disciplined when necessary, and loved as much as I could. I laughed with my children and cherished all the funny, touching and silly things they did and said. For me, in the experience of this life, motherhood will always rank number one.

Ned and I always told our children to dream big. To go for it and do great things. Having heeded that advice, now the children I had cherished spending time with at home were slowly leaving us to venture out on their own to do those great things. Sadly, I couldn't keep them home forever.

This time, the early 1980s, was a watershed period for me. The nest certainly wasn't empty yet: Jackie, 16, and Peter, 10, were still living under our roof. But the ranks had thinned from five to two, and it was starting to fully sink in for me: The chaotic and blissful poppity-pop chapter—with five young children in motion—was over for good. Those glory days of motherhood with all my children bouncing off the walls at home and going different directions was only a snapshot frozen in time, forever preserved in my memory, and still treasured just as much today as I write this at age 86. My children's benevolence and capacity for good, with me as their mom and Ned as their father, is my creative stamp on the world that will outlive my time here. That they are each happy, healthy and productive—and most important, kind souls—is the most bountiful gift I could ever want in this life.

So, as the nest started to empty and I looked ahead to my own next chapter, little did I know that it would formulate around hand-painted cowboy hats, in the West's most Western town, Scottsdale.

Julie and Patrick.

— Chapter Seven —

RANGER RESOURCES

UNDER THE COVER OF DARKNESS, I worked my way up the rocky outcrop formed roughly fourteen million years ago. The impressive curved arms of saguaro cacti were stark silhouettes against the early morning sky before 5 a.m. My flashlight beam bounced across the other varieties of cactus: barrel, jumping cholla and prickly pear. Spidery ocotillo fingers spiraled toward the sky. Five years after arriving in Arizona, I was a fully converted transplant, rising in the darkness to beat the brutal desert sun and prowling the rocky trail along with so many gila monsters, horned lizards and chuckwallas. A hawk silently glided overhead as the milky light of dawn first cracked open the horizon. The desert—especially in summer—was still alive as the night gave way to day. To understand I was an observer on this trail, and also the observed—perhaps by a western diamondback rattlesnake curled in a rock crevice as I passed—was an energizing feeling to begin my day.

Shady

The ragged silhouette of Squaw Peak (later renamed Piestewa Peak, in 2008, to honor the first American Indian woman to die in combat while serving in the U.S. military) became a comforting presence and my new marker, in the way rolling green hillsides once had been in Pennsylvania and Michigan. On some mornings the yips of bone-thin coyotes echoed to me as I climbed Summit Trail #300, a 2.2-mile urban hike that was always both heavily trafficked and a taxing climb that got my blood coursing and oxygen pumping.

This had become my new exercise routine not by insanity, but rather necessity. Yes, being on the trail every morning at 4:45 a.m. with flashlight in hand helped me beat the desert heat. During the winter, however, it meant bracing against cold dry temperatures in the thirties and forties, which in my Michigan years had been considered balmy and jacket-optional. There is no question one adapts to the climate, whether hot or cold.

More importantly, the daily hike got me up, moving and ready for my day, because my weeks were full as the owner of my own company: Ranger Resources. Concerned friends would ask whether, as a 50-year-old woman by herself, I was concerned I would run into a bad man at that odd hour in the darkness. To which I'd reply, "I've been looking for one for years, and haven't had any luck!"

Since I had no business background, my morning hike gave me time to think and brainstorm. I had fallen into this groove, hiking to the top and back and then picking up a bagel and cup of coffee by 6:00 a.m., to start each day. My daily mini-expedition matched what I had done in the business world, striking out on my own and discovering something that put me in my element. I had gone from having only a vague idea to now calling on people at all the major resort hotels, primarily in Scottsdale and Paradise Valley. I was an accidental entrepreneur, and loving every minute of it.

My new venture started to formulate toward the end of 1983 as the size of our household dwindled. Once the children started leaving for college and the household size shrank, it was never quite the same.

Fewer children at home meant fewer demands on my time. I knew I wasn't cut out to fill my days strolling through shopping malls, going out to lunch and playing bridge. I was determined to find something productive, and began pondering different possibilities. As I did so, an obscure California company quietly released its now-iconic "1984" television commercial introducing the Apple Macintosh personal computer. The company ran the advertisement in just a handful of local markets, on December 31, 1983, just before midnight. Most of us first saw British athlete Anya Major hurtling the hammer at Big Brother a month later during Super Bowl XVIII. If only I had been prescient enough to buy some stock back then in Apple, a company that would go on to revolutionize personal electronics with the iPod, iPad and 1.5 billion iPhones manufactured in total only twelve years after its initial release. In my humble little corner of the economic universe, to start my own business I began by focusing on what I knew: that I was living in a world-class tourism destination with Scottsdale and Paradise Valley at the epicenter of the resort trade in metropolitan Phoenix, a.k.a. the Valley of the Sun.

Synchronously, around this same time I met an artist who hand-painted cowboy hats. Something clicked as I began to formulate the equation: tourist destination plus resort hospitality plus Western art and apparel. When I added that up, my business model crystallized: With the endless schedule of conferences, events and golf tournaments unfolding right where I lived, there would be ongoing demand by organizers for bulk quantities of Western items for attendees. I could provide one-stop shopping for whatever an event organizer might need for their attendees: cowboy hats, bandannas and any other classic Western accoutrements, including high-end gifts for meeting planners.

Ned was very supportive of my idea and encouraged me to plunge ahead, so I did just that by starting to get connected with convention and business bureaus. First I needed a name, and came up with Ranger Resources, which had a nice alliterative ring and highlighted my business solution as an advertising specialty company with access to

"Mile by mile, life's a trial.
Yard by yard, it's not so hard.
Inch by inch, it's a cinch."

–Proverb

any amenity or product, from pencils to high-end $5,000 gifts.

In April 1984 I launched the business from home, and what a year it was—one that would give us the launch of *Jeopardy!* with longtime host Alex Trebek, the Summer Olympics on U.S. soil in Los Angeles, and Arnold Schwarzenegger as the Terminator. My first step was developing my plan. I would need to tap decision-makers in the hospitality industry and get connected to groups planning conventions in Arizona. I targeted the convention bureaus in Scottsdale, Phoenix and Tucson, which paid big dividends. By joining each, I received a twelve-month planning calendar listing every group planning an event, with a contact name and phone number. I hired a designer, who created a logo incorporating a cactus with a red cowboy hat, and a brochure. I'd throw in a load of laundry and then venture out to my scheduled meetings with planners at hotels. I was not intimidated or fearful, but rather energized: I really enjoyed calling on people to tell them about Ranger Resources. I quickly learned that the gold standard was getting to the meeting planner and director of purchasing at each resort property.

I recruited my son Patrick, who was attending UofA in Tucson, to call on resort hotels there while I worked the wider Phoenix market. When he graduated two years later, with a degree in Spanish and a minor in English, he would go full-time as the general manager of Ranger Resources. Patrick was very good at detail work; I hated it. We were a dynamic mother-son duo: It only took a couple weeks to get our first customer. One day I answered the phone and heard a male voice.

"This is Rick Miller with the Boys and Girls Club. I want to order a gross of hats."

I thought it was a friend of mine who was joking around. So I said, "Yeah, and I'm Mae West."

After a brief pause, he said, "No, seriously. I would like to order a gross of hats."

"Oh right, of course," I said, scrambling. "One moment please." I turned to Patrick, put my hand over the receiver and said, "He wants a gross of cowboy hats. What's a gross?"

Patrick whispered, "One hundred and forty-four."

With that, Ranger Resources was on the map! The month after I started the business, Jackie graduated from Xavier College Preparatory and followed her sibling tradition of attending UofA. She went to college on a full tennis scholarship.

In October, after six months working from home, Ranger Resources moved out of the house into a small commercial space at 4221 N. Winfield Scott Plaza in Scottsdale. The 1,000 square feet had three rooms, including one with a conference table. Orders started to come more frequently, and got larger, too. The director of purchasing at a major Phoenix resort called and ordered 144 gross of hats. I'd gone from not knowing what a "gross" was to fulfilling a huge order of more than 20,000 hats. We bought a white work van with no windows and emblazoned our "Ranger Resources" logo on both sides.

In 1986, we all began the year by mourning the terrible Space Shuttle Challenger disaster in January, which killed the crew of seven, including schoolteacher Christa McAuliffe, when the craft disintegrated just seventy-three seconds after launch. Four months later Patrick and Julie (liberal arts) both graduated from UofA, the same month some five million people joined hands to form a continuous human chain, aptly dubbed "Hands Across America," from New York to California, to raise money to alleviate hunger and homelessness. It was special, unusual and exciting for Ned and me to celebrate two of our children graduating from college in the same year, a synchronicity normally reserved for the parents of twins. Julie had caught up to her older brother because he had taken five years instead of four. As I mentioned, once Patrick graduated, he worked with me full-time as the Ranger Resources general manager. He also made all our deliveries. Truly, Patrick was a godsend. I never would have been able to run my business as successfully without Patrick by my side. As the general manager, he helmed our daily morning meeting and kept tabs on every detail. That allowed me to flit about and make calls, because I knew he never let any important detail slip through the cracks. I could have never succeeded without him. And, of course, it was so much fun to work side by side with him for what would be a total of thirteen years. We enjoyed countless lunches together at Side Door and The Sugar Bowl, and traveled to all the gift exhibition shows together.

In the meantime, we had also added four other employees to spread the workload. When the phone rang, we all snapped to action. Part of the excitement was that we never knew who might call. In those days before email, cellphones, texting and all the rest, our orders came in the old-fashioned way, with the ring of the office phone and either a voice call or a facsimile transmission (look it up, grandchildren). Hotels and convention groups formed the bulk of our business.

The early months of operation, April to October 1984, were slow with very few calls and only sporadic orders. Most of our calls were outgoing, to set up appointments. Directors of purchasing at major resort properties were busy people; we couldn't just show up unannounced and expect to see them at the drop of a hat. They were also besieged with all sorts of salespeople offering every type of hospitality product and service, from commercial kitchen equipment to pillow-soft Egyptian cotton bath towels. We were competing with every other supplier for the time and attention of these busy decision-makers.

Then, slowly, the phone started to ring more, especially as we moved toward our first tourist season, with January to May being the prime months in Arizona. Soon there was rarely a day when an order or two didn't come in from someone. On an average day, once it got busy, we were out delivering our Western wares for four or five hours each day throughout metropolitan Phoenix. We were providing products for a number of events hosted by Fortune 500 companies, with groups ranging from twenty-five up to 2,000.

Our least expensive offering was our standard cowboy hat, with two stock versions. One had a vinyl band that we could customize

Snady

Tom (L), Edward, Ned, Peter, Patrick, Julie (L), me and Jackie.

with printing for the specific client. Our more expensive items included custom framed photographs, Stetson hats, Southwest tiles and fancy bolo ties with embedded turquoise. We created lots of gift baskets for guest rooms, which usually had a strong Southwest flavor including custom-branded salsa and Arizona yucca candy. One client wanted tarantula paperweights. Although I'd never once seen one on all my hikes, I knew they were desert dwellers who conjured the ruggedness of the West. So we found the tarantula paperweights.

Patrick and I attended an annual gift show in Dallas, where we'd spend three days sourcing new products. In our business we were the middleman between product manufacturers and our resort property clients. The more unique and interesting items we could source, the better. As I continued my daily 4:45 a.m. routine up the trail every morning, Edward hit the educational trifecta in 1987. He graduated with his Juris Doctor (JD) from ASU, earned his master's degree from Thunderbird School of Global Management, and passed the Arizona Bar examination. That same year our youngest, Peter, started at Brophy College Preparatory as a freshman.

The next year Jackie graduated from UofA with a degree in English. Edward moved to Mexico City in 1989, where he enrolled in Mexican law school: Universidad Nacional Autónoma de México (UNAM), in Mexico City. Julie, our oldest daughter, was our first child to get married. She married Thomas Frederick Adelson on June 4, 1988, at Brophy College Chapel in Phoenix. Ned walked her down the aisle and this was a monumental day for us both, seeing our first child get married. We enjoyed the reception at the Schumacher estate on the north side of Mummy Mountain in Paradise Valley.

That same year Ned and his partner decided to sell the plane. They both agreed that perhaps the luster of excitement and novelty had worn off, especially when balanced against the ongoing cost of maintenance and storage. As busy as we all were, neither of them was using the plane for more than a few hours a month.

As the decade drew to a close, 1989 was a fundamental turning point both in geopolitical history and in the Ranger household. On the larger front, a wave of revolutions swept the old Eastern Bloc in Europe, a movement that would culminate with the overthrow of communist dictatorships, the dismantling of the Berlin Wall and the dissolution of the Soviet Union. Change was the new world order, and that matched the transition for Ned and me. We did not have to look far, only to 1991, to see the next chapter of our lives looming as empty-nesters. Four of our children had graduated college, Edward from law school as well, and Julie was married. When Peter graduated from Brophy College Prep in 1991, that would be it: All our children would be out of the house and on their own.

This impending reality, however, did not strike a melancholy chord in me. Sure, I had moments of nostalgia recalling when the children were all younger and at home—poppity pop!—and there's nothing quite like being at the epicenter of a busy household with young children. It was simply the best of times. However, I've never liked to wallow in regret or looking backward. Instead, I was excited about what the next chapter would hold for each of my children. When I arose at 4:15 a.m. each morning to make my way to the dark trail, I first thanked God immediately after waking up. I lived a blessed life. I was the luckiest person in the whole world, because I loved my family and I know they loved me. I had my own business, and it was going gangbusters. I was getting paid to help people throw parties and host fabulous events, and I got to work with my son Patrick every day. I was ready for "The Golden Years" with Ned, whatever that meant.

− Chapter Eight −

MEXICAN JAILBREAK

BY 1994, NED AND I WERE CLOSE TO BEING EMPTY-NESTERS, and the time had come to downsize. It was hard to believe that, somehow, fifteen years had passed in the house that had been our landing spot for our new life in the desert.

The year had begun with a tabloid drama that started in January, which would play out like a TV installment whodunnit, when low-level hitman Shane Stant whacked Nancy Kerrigan's right leg with a twenty-one inch collapsible baton. Eventually we learned that he and his uncle had been contracted by Jeff Gillooly (you can't make this stuff up), the ex-husband of Kerrigan's skating rival Tonya Harding, and Harding's bodyguard, Shawn Eckhardt. Harding would only later confess, in 2018, that she knew "something was up" in the plot to take out her longtime rival who was the primary obstacle to Harding making the Olympic team.

During the early years of the 1990s we marked many milestones in the Ranger household that cumulatively became a blur of seminal events.

125

Shady

On June 26, 1990, the temperature in Phoenix hit an unbelievable 122 degrees. In an odd aside, add up those numbers denoting the date—6, 26 and 90—and it totals the same as the record temperature that day: 122. It was so hot that Sky Harbor International Airport closed for a short time because aircraft could not achieve sufficient lift in such kiln-like conditions. On that day I took my five children outside, where we cracked an egg on the driveway at our house on Naumann Drive in Paradise Valley. Indeed, the egg fried and would leave a yellow yolk stain we'd never be able to fully scrub from the concrete.

In 1991, Peter graduated from Brophy College Prep in Phoenix and was awarded a Flinn Foundation full-ride scholarship, which only twenty Arizona high school graduates received each year. The aim was to keep at least some of Arizona's shining academic stars in state by providing four years of study at an Arizona public university, including a funded internship, personal mentorship by faculty and alumni scholars, and other benefits. Peter bucked the family tradition, after his four siblings had all chosen the University of Arizona, by choosing Barrett Honors College at Arizona State University, including one year studying abroad.

On June 1 that year, Ned and I welcomed our first grandchildren, Grace Ann and Thomas James Adelson—twins, courtesy of our daughter Julie and her husband Tom. What a joy it was for Ned and me to spend time with these twins. We took them to the Melting Pot restaurant when they were three months old, and to Costco. We just couldn't get enough of them!

ON September 21, Jackie married Terence (Terry) Michael Flood at Brophy College Chapel in Phoenix and had the reception at the Registry Resort on Scottsdale Road. With that, two of our children were married (our two girls) and four were out of college.

On January 9, 1993, we went from record heat to record rain, which washed out the Mill Avenue bridge and sent tons of garbage and concrete from the bridge and a landfill cascading down the Salt River. It took three months to rebuild the bridge. I was actually right there, one block away, to watch the raging waters collapse the bridge, which brought an eerie feeling of being absolutely helpless to do anything to stop the ravaging damage. The year had begun with Bill Clinton giving his first inaugural address. Our son Edward had a hand in Clinton's presidency. Living in Mexico since the early 1990s, Edward was president of the group Democrats Abroad in Mexico. He had been chosen in 1992 as the delegate from that group for the Democratic Party National Convention in New York City. In turn, he had voted for Bill Clinton's nomination. Subsequently, in 1993 Edward graduated with his Mexican law degree (Licenciatura de Derecho) and started Mexico's first environmental law firm, coinciding with passage of the North American Free Trade Agreement (NAFTA). That experience at the Democratic National Convention would not be Edward's last foray into politics.

Again, I could not believe almost forty years had passed since I had seen another young upstart Democrat, John F. Kennedy, whose campaign rolled through Michigan in 1960 as I watched him ride down Woodward Avenue sitting on the back of an open convertible. Back then I was at the end of my first pregnancy and just weeks away from becoming a mother for the first time with Edward. Now, in 1994, all five of our children were grown and moving through the world on their own.

By 1994, Ranger Resources was still going strong, as was my fruitless search for a bad man on the dark trail every morning up Squaw Peak, which all led to the official end of our time in the house on Naumann Drive; we sold it—complete with the yellow yolk stain from our egg experiment—on March 30, 1994. We had been the eighth residents to move into the neighborhood, and had owned the house just two months shy of fifteen years, so it was bittersweet to close that chapter. We had arrived in Arizona with five children who were all now young adults. Ned and I moved to Briarwood V in Scottsdale, lot

#81 at 5696 N. 73rd Street. It was a slump block ranch house, with long, skinny white-washed bricks. We had a swimming pool.

By 1995, Ned had semi-retired and transitioned to working from a home office under the banner "The Ranger Law Firm." Fully established and with all our children just about through college, he didn't have to work as many hours as he once did. He found it more comfortable to work at home. That May Peter graduated from ASU Barrett Honors College, which made us official empty-nesters. Edward, Julie, Patrick and Jackie had all earned bachelor's degrees from University of Arizona in Tucson; Peter was the lone Sun Devil in the family with his degree from Arizona State University in Interdisciplinary Studies. In addition, Edward had earned two law degrees, from ASU and Universidad Nacional Autónoma de México, and was living in Mexico City. Two months later we welcomed our third grandchild, John Patrick Hutt, who was born July 27.

Two years later, 1997 became a watershed year for the entire family when representatives of the Democratic Senatorial Campaign Committee approached Edward and asked if he'd be willing to run against two-term incumbent Senator John McCain in the 1998 election. Of course, they hadn't just picked Edward from the phone book: He was well-established within the Democratic Party as the leader of Democrats Abroad in Mexico and as the group's delegate to the 1992 convention. Still Edward was leery, because at the time McCain was at the apex of his popularity, including support from a lot of Democrats, and well-branded as the outlaw Western maverick who cut against the grain and walked his own path. But as Edward realized, and the local *Phoenix New Times* pointed out, McCain was not completely invulnerable to criticism: "… absent from their coverage has been the McCain familiar to his Arizona constituents as something of a… scalawag, to be kind. Magically, all of McCain's political liabilities have evaporated, replaced in print by a brand-spanking-new treasury of virtues."

Edward rightly asked his suitors: Why spend more than a year of his life running an uphill campaign that almost certainly would end in defeat? Why was he the anointed one to take on the almost impossible task of unseating McCain? The party leaders replied that the Democratic Party needed a candidate who was both credible and had a strong foundation in both Arizona and Mexico, the critical foreign neighbor to the south. Edward checked all those boxes, including being fluent in Spanish. He took some time to consider the offer and talked to local political heavyweights such as former Phoenix mayor Terry Goddard, attorney general Grant Woods and Janet Napolitano, who would become the twenty-first governor of Arizona in 2003. Eventually Edward decided to go for it. While McCain staked his claim to the maverick title, Edward, too, had often gone against prevailing wisdom. He had migrated south from America to Mexico City to find a job when most people go the other way. He never lacked confidence or optimism, and saw running for the U.S. Senate as a once-in-a-lifetime opportunity. And while it would certainly be a longshot gambit, he knew he couldn't win if he didn't get in the game. He sold his law practice in Mexico City and moved back to Arizona. The proceeds from the sale of his practice became the initial funds for his U.S. Senate campaign run.

There was no doubt this would be a David v. Goliath undertaking. However, it also carried a vague hint of possibility, as Jesse "The Body" Ventura, a former World Wrestling Federation wrestler, was running for governor of Minnesota in the same election cycle. If a C-list actor (see *Predator*) could run for the governorship of a state, why not the bilingual Edward Ranger for U.S. Senate?

Party affiliation in Arizona at the time broke down as roughly evenly split: thirty-five percent each for Democrats and Republicans, with a strong Independent base of thirty percent. To win, Edward would have to carve into that thirty percent not already officially entrenched in the two main parties. However, in name recognition and as a political commodity in Arizona, Edward essentially began at zero. His only initial boost came courtesy of our strong family surname, "Ranger," which was a rugged-minded moniker against his supposed maverick foe. "Edward Ranger" sounded like a guy who could roll up his shirt sleeves, chew tobacco and be the sheriff in any Arizona county; ours was a good name for an Arizona politician of any stripe.

One of Edward's prominent platform positions was that Arizona needed a strong leader who was not so woefully and willfully ignorant of Arizona's most important neighbor to the south. No one in state leadership, he noted, could speak Spanish. Or read the Mexican Constitution, which is based on civil law tradition rather than common law as in the U.S.

To be certain, this was going to be a shoestring campaign run solely by family members. I had the stately title of liaison to the Democratic Party of Arizona. Edward's two sisters, Julie and Jackie, who were both well-connected and could network moneyed families, would head up fundraising. Patrick would oversee ground operations, and Peter was the strategist and interface with the Democratic Party at the national level. Ned, in his semi-retirement, would be Edward's consigliere in all other matters and primary travel partner to share time behind the wheel of the official campaign vehicle, a leased Chevy Suburban.

Edward set the campaign tone with a few simple goals: have fun, live within our means on the campaign trail and, in the end, represent

Democrats and Arizona well no matter the outcome. Another goal was to visit every one of the fifteen counties in the state at least once; these counties sprawled across 113,998 square miles and incorporated cities, towns, mountains, deserts, forests, tribal lands and high plains. Thus began a whirlwind family adventure as Edward launched and engaged in a statewide campaign to become a U.S. Senator from Arizona. True to his word, he and Ned visited every county in the state, traveling to the larger population centers outside metropolitan Phoenix, Tucson and Flagstaff, and numerous smaller outposts. Each week Edward and Ned set up a schedule based around events throughout the state. If there was a parade in Winslow, an art show in Prescott or a harvest festival in Yuma, that's where they'd be that week—because those events would draw all the local dignitaries and most of the area population. They'd jump in the leased Suburban and share a single room at a cut-rate motel to save money.

And money—or more accurately, a lack of money—was always an issue. With the funds Edward put in from the sale of his firm plus all the donors combined, we still only raised about $250,000 total. McCain, meanwhile, enjoyed the largesse of tens of millions of dollars, most of which he knew he didn't have to spend against his universally unknown opponent. McCain was a political powerhouse who could host a Saturday night tablecloth event and haul in $500,000, while my son and husband were sharing a dingy room at Motel 6.

And yet, their time on the road afforded father and son a unique time to bond, talk about life and enjoy Arizona's spectacular sunrises and sunsets from every unique vantage point in the state. They listened to a lot of country music while they drove, and adopted Roger Miller's "King of the Road" as their official anthem.

They'd roll into small-town Arizona and stop at the nearest radio station—and TV stations in the larger enclaves—knowing our other children had already done the advance work to schedule the appearance. Indeed, it was a big deal when a candidate for U.S. Senate rolled into Eloy, Wickenburg, Payson and all the other towns. Then they'd hit city hall, the Rotary Club and local chamber of commerce.

"The greatest glory in living lies not in never falling, but in rising every time we fall."

–Nelson Mandela

They'd land at people's houses and spend evenings in living rooms talking to small groups about Edward's vision for the state. They would show up unannounced at tribal council meetings, where the members were always impressed that the young candidate had brought his father. That gave Edward immediate credibility in their eyes. In towns and tribal lands near the border, Edward often delivered his entire speech, and took questions, in Spanish. Then they'd grab another cheap motel room or stay with friends. Or sometimes they'd skip any accommodations altogether and drive through the night to arrive in the next town for the early morning radio show. They knocked on doors and coordinated with other Democratic candidates to bolster those efforts.

Meanwhile, in May I had sold Ranger Resources, and a few months later I earned my real estate license along with my son Patrick. We had a good run with the business, but I was ready to try something new without the daily commitment and responsibility of owning and operating a business. That fall, Jackie called to tell me that she'd discovered Bikram Yoga (hot yoga). She told me she thought I would love it. I just wondered how she had time to discover a new form of yoga while fundraising for her brother's campaign for the U.S. Senate.

I tried hot yoga a couple times and thought it was interesting. During my second class, which I took with Jackie, I was in the back row staring ahead toward the big mirror, the people on either side of me staring at me. Wow, I thought, I must be doing really well for a beginner, because all eyes are on me! Then when I looked more closely at the mirror, I discovered what had drawn everyone's gaze. In the 110-degree room, my face was covered with a ghastly white foam: I had not considered that the extreme temperatures and exertion would convert my daily moisture cream into this scary concoction. Instead, everyone thought I was having a seizure, with many poised to dial 9-1-1.

"Oh my God, Mother," Jackie said, laughing. "I can't take you anywhere."

This was the inauspicious beginning to the journey that would take me into the realm of hot yoga as a certified instructor and recipient of the Mahatma Award, which represented being the most inspirational student, handed to me by the founder himself, Bikram Choudhury. That I would go on such an adventure would have seemed impossible to me that day after I'd contorted myself into a foamy-faced mess.

ON January 22, 1998, our son Patrick's first daughter, Caroline Palmer Ranger, was born. The birth marked a glorious milestone for Ned and me, our fourth grandchild. The joyous occasion was a stark contrast to the great loss that would follow us through the rest of the year. On April 8, on Wednesday during Holy Week, our daughter Jackie's husband Terry Flood died. He had been battling Hodgkin's lymphoma and had received a bone marrow transplant as part of his treatment. On the day Terry died, he said he'd love to taste one last pizza from Chris Bianco, the legendary proprietor of Pizzeria Bianco, who had only honored one similar last request.

The funeral, on the day after Easter, was a full house at St. Thomas the Apostle in Phoenix, a day of sadness, grief and reflection. That he had been diagnosed in 1990 and lived so many more years was little consolation, especially with a type of cancer that had a very high survival rate. Ned had even warned Jackie that she could find herself a young widow. To see one's child lose a spouse was devastating for us as parents.

With Jackie grieving, I stepped up my role to help Edward with his campaign that summer. For our first appointment, in a remote blip somewhere in the sprawling Navajo Nation, we arrived an hour late. This was squarely my fault, because I hadn't factored in that unlike the rest of Arizona, this autonomous territory uses Daylight Saving Time. Nonetheless, I think we had Edward at every parade held anywhere in the state of Arizona in 1997 and 1998, and we were meeting our goal of having a lot of fun along the way. Edward hammered home his message of "Arizona First," which was a jab at McCain's ever-present and wistful gaze toward the U.S. presidency. In contrast, Edward positioned himself as the candidate focused on Arizona and the state's relationship with Mexico. Meanwhile, the *Phoenix New Times* was taking potshots at the challenger by putting Edward on its cover and mocking his effort as a low-budget family affair. Even so, despite the challenges, we had managed to produce a television spot; it showed a political campaign button: "John McCain for President." Then, when the button spun to reveal the other side, it was stamped "John McCain for U.S. Senate." The intended message was that he was running for Senate only to bolster his chances to run for president. We were amateurs at running a political campaign, only later would we all agree the TV spot was a bit weird, at best—and, most likely, pretty horrible. I think we had enough budget to run it once, on PBS at 2 a.m., to ensure that no one actually saw it. In the days before online access to everything, I think the spot ran that one time and then vaporized into the ether of the forgettable, never to be seen again.

As the campaign continued into the summer of 1998, we just were not getting any traction. Edward had repeatedly challenged McCain's campaign manager Larry Pike—who coincidentally we knew because he had been our neighbor in Grosse Pointe, Michigan—to schedule some debates between the two candidates. But with McCain's solid lead in the polls there was no incentive to debate, and the campaign simply ignored Edward's pleas. So we sent out a press release to provoke McCain and called him a coward in print; i.e., Come on, Mr. Maverick War Hero: Why are you so scared to debate this nobody Democrat who's basically broke and running a U.S. Senate campaign staffed solely by family members? It actually worked, and we got three head-to-head debates, in Phoenix, Flagstaff and Tucson, that aired on PBS. We also brought in a heavyweight fundraiser from Washington D.C. who urged us to devote hours a day to "call time," which meant taking all our Rolodexes (again, for my grandchildren: Google it!) and cold-calling every contact we had to ask for funds. Edward spent six hours a day on the phone asking people for money, and then traveled with Ned in the afternoons. Despite the D.C. fundraiser's best recommendations, Edward's own maverick streak shined through again. He didn't want to spend the last months of the campaign groveling for money. He had set out to have fun, and cold-calling people and pleading for them to cut checks was no fun. Instead, he said it was time to leave it all on the table by hitting the road hard and making a final push to meet voters face-to-face where they lived. It was that renegade spirit that led to the great Mexican jailbreak of 1998.

After yet another campaign event and speech, Ned, Edward and Peter had some open hours. They were in Southern Arizona, in Nogales, and looking for something to do, which meant finding a creative way to kill some time that would simultaneously benefit the campaign. That's when they heard a story on the radio about an Arizonan who had been arrested, across the border in Mexico, for having some .22 caliber rounds in his trunk. Despite the man's protestations that he had simply forgotten the rounds were in the trunk after a range session some weeks prior, in Mexican law there was no component of intent: The man was guilty of a felony and locked up.

"Oh, man, this could be our opportunity," Edward exclaimed to his father and youngest brother.

"What are you talking about?" my husband asked as he navigated the Suburban down a narrow Nogales street.

"Dad, I'm a Mexican lawyer. I have my national Mexican law credential with me. It will be an adventure."

"What will be an adventure?" Peter asked from the back seat, wondering if his oldest brother was dizzy from the heat, bad diner food and too much road time.

"What I'm saying is let's go bust this guy out of jail!" Edward said.

Ned and Peter didn't know what to say. They did have hours available, and Edward's enthusiasm was palpable. Yet this seemed like a big leap.

"Come on guys, let's do it!" Edward said.

"What the hell," Ned said, smiling.

"I'm in," Peter said.

"Now," Ned said, "which way to the border?"

After crossing into Mexico and finding the jail, Edward climbed out of the Suburban, threw on his suit jacket (no tie), slammed the door and motioned for his dad to put down the passenger window. Edward leaned into the air-conditioned comfort of the American-made rig.

"I don't know how long I'll be in there. If I'm not back in four hours, call the American consulate to come get me out. And keep these doors locked."

With that grim send-off, he turned and walked into the jail, showing his Mexican lawyer credential to the guard behind bulletproof glass. In perfect Spanish, Edward said he was there to see the American they had, and that he was his abogado, his lawyer. The guard picked up a phone, spoke, nodded a few times and then pushed a button that buzzed open the door.

Edward went through a seemingly never-ending series of these encounters, more guards behind more thick glass and more doors buzzed open as he descended into the bowels of the Mexican prison. As he did so it got hotter, darker and louder. Finally, Edward was let into a large holding cell with some 150 Mexicans staring at him as the door clanked shut behind him.

"I'm here for the American arrested for having bullets at the border," he said in Spanish. There was a round of murmurs and commotion, but no response. The dingy lighting didn't help: Edward couldn't see much in the far corners of the dank cell.

"Is there an American here?" he yelled in English.

Then he saw an arm go up and a man step from the shadows. Edward, who could feel his shirt soaking through with sweat, slowly pushed himself through the tight crowd of the accused and convicted until he reached the man, his new client.

"Are you the one who had the .22 rounds in your trunk?"

The man nodded. He looked scared, disoriented and tired. "Do you have any water?"

"We'll sort that out. Look, I'm a lawyer licensed in both the U.S. and Mexico. Let me see what I can do to help you. Plus, I'm running for U.S. Senate. Maybe you heard?"

The man looked puzzled.

"I'm Ed Ranger. Running against John McCain."

"I know McCain."

"You and everyone else. Well, anyway, let's make this an international incident and get you sprung."

The man nodded, but he looked positively broken. Edward could sense the circle of inmates tightening around them as the level of noise and commotion started to crescendo. Edward thought about his father and brother waiting in the Suburban and wondered if they, too, might get swept up and thrown in the same cell just for good measure. Then he wondered if this was all a bad idea and a bit grandiose. Just when he thought he might get assaulted by the angry mob, the cell went deadly silent. Then the sound of footsteps marching in unison—a firing squad, perhaps? Suddenly four uniformed troopers were pointing assault rifles at Edward and his bewildered client.

"Warden wants to see you," one of the guards barked in Spanish. "Ahora!"

Edward tried to console his client: "I'll be back."

The guards marched Edward back through the labyrinth of long hallways and locked doors as they ascended to a bright, airy floor with ice-cold AC. The warden's office was as nice as any corporate executive suite Edward had ever seen, and replete with a bird's-eye view of the sprawling prison grounds and razor-wire-topped walls around the perimeter. Edward stepped forward and shook the warden's hand.

He eyed the American suspiciously and then said in Spanish, "Who the (expletive) are you, and what are you doing in my prison?"

"Well," Edward said in the warden's native tongue, "I am your worst nightmare."

"What?"

"That's right. I'm Edward Ranger, an American lawyer licensed to practice law in Mexico. And I'm running for U.S. Senate."

The warden shrugged his shoulders. More than a year on the road with every Ranger family member on deck had obviously not moved the name-recognition needle much.

"Well, I'm sure you know Senator John McCain. He's my opponent."

The warden nodded. "Why are you here?"

"I'm here to get my client out."

"What?"

"Look, you have no idea what trouble you're going to face when I call a press conference to talk about this innocent man being arrested on a bogus charge when we both know it was just an oversight on his part."

The warden's posture had softened: He was listening.

"Let's work this out," Edward said. "If I were you I'd just get rid of this guy. You don't need the spotlight and all that comes with it."

Edward had made his play. He let the silence hang there. He wondered why the four guards still had their rifles aimed at him.

"OK," the warden said. "We'll figure it out."

Then the guards marched Edward back through the maze that descended to the dim, hot holding cell, where Edward delivered the good news to his client. Three hours later, the guards came back, retrieved Edward and marched him back to the entrance. They opened the door and Edward saw the light of freedom again, and his father and brother waiting in the Suburban.

"The warden's going to make the decision," the guard said. "We'll work it out on our own schedule."

Then they motioned Edward out, and he watched them slam the door shut. Edward walked to the Suburban, climbed in and relayed his tale. With that ostensibly done, they decided they were all famished and went to find some good Mexican food.

As it turned out, the warden was more astute than Edward had thought: He released the American that very day, at 11:55 p.m., by discreetly having a plainclothes guard walk him back across the border. No crowds, no daylight, no show of force and no time to coordinate press coverage on either side of the border. Edward had indeed, sprung his client, but ultimately, he got no credit for the effort in the press or anywhere else. For our family, it didn't matter. How many times in life can you break someone out of a Mexican jail, without any violence, and live to tell the story for the rest of your life?

And Ned especially—a lawyer himself and a mentor to his son—thought the entire experience was wonderful because it embodied the power of the law. And in his version, the power of a Mexican law license held by his American son. That would make the time together, as father and two sons, especially poignant as a crowning moment in Ned's affinity for the law and his life, too, because weeks later he would be gone.

— Chapter Nine —

FAREWELL

THE BEGINNING OF THE END CAME at a fundraiser for Edward's campaign in late August 1998. Good friends of Edward had offered to host the event at their home in Rio Verde, which was thirty miles from Scottsdale. We eagerly accepted the invite, because we were eagerly fundraising and yet never seemed to be able to add a significant amount to the campaign coffers. During Edward's speech at that event, Ned leaned over to me with a look of distress.

"I'm not feeling well," he said. "We need to go."

As we tiptoed toward the front door I stopped to whisper to the hostess why we were leaving early. Edward was preoccupied and didn't notice as we quietly left and went home. The next morning Edward came over early to see how Ned was doing. However, he was still not feeling well, with labored breathing. I called the rest of the family. By the time everyone arrived, Ned's condition had worsened, and we realized it was time to call for an ambulance.

At the hospital with all our family present, after an examination, doctors whisked Ned away for immediate triple-bypass heart surgery. The immediate surgery was successful, and Ned recovered at the hospital for a couple days before coming home. Once he was back home, we were all optimistic about a full recovery and were encouraged the surgery had gone so well. Then, in a shocking turn, five days later Ned had an aneurysm that caused a blood clot to break loose. He would never fully come back to us; an ambulance once again rushed him to the hospital. As Ned floated in and out of consciousness, we each took time to whisper our final messages of love to him. Edward McDonald Ranger passed away peacefully on September 9, 1998, surrounded by his family at Scottsdale Memorial South Hospital.

Post-mortem, the doctors discovered scar tissue on half of Ned's heart. He had suffered a heart attack about ten years prior, with no surgery, that apparently had left this considerable scar tissue on the heart. This discovery explained a lot for us; poor Ned had been laboring for a decade with only about fifty percent usage of his heart. That physical struggle, including labored breathing, explained some changes we'd all noticed in Ned's personality the last few years of his life. It gave us all a new empathy for what a struggle it had been for him.

When Ned died we were all heartbroken. Our family patriarch was gone, the only child of nine in his family to be born an American. The hard-working kid who grew up on Cadillac Boulevard in Detroit, knew he wanted to be a lawyer and crawled out of bed every weekday morning at 4 a.m. to go sling scrambled eggs and hash browns for the hardened factory workers coming off the night shift at the Chrysler plant. The American kid who had cemented his place in the Motor City milieu and gone on to a distinguished career as a lawyer.

Ned's death put into perspective that even a campaign for U.S. Senate was less important than it had seemed throughout 1997 and most of 1998. Still, Ned himself would not have stood for us quitting less than two months from the finish line. We would pay our respects and then carry on with Edward's final push to election day.

In the proper Irish tradition, we needed to plan both a wake and a proper Catholic mass. We were all surprised when Edward's "Mexican Jailbreak" client crashed the wake and, along with his wife, lifted a glass to the father of the man who had plucked him from those dark confines. The memorial and mass were at Brophy College Chapel on September 14. Many of Ned's cousins came from Philadelphia, along with other relatives and a large turnout of friends and legal peers. Several days later after a torrential rainstorm, the entire extended family was at Jackie's house, in the backyard, when a double rainbow broke through the clouds. Jackie's son Jack, 2, pointed and said that was his father and grandfather looking down on him. There was not a dry adult eye in the crowd.

AFTER hiking Squaw Peak in the dark for fifteen years, in May 1998 I decided to see if I could get reservations for two at Phantom Ranch at the bottom of the Grand Canyon. After booking it, I called Jackie and asked her to join me on the hike. With Ned's passing, we both wondered if we should cancel the trip—and then realized again that Ned would have never stood for such a move. Instead, Jackie and I

Celebration of Life

of

Edward McDonald Ranger

"NED"

October 15, 1929 - September 9, 1998

Memorial Mass
Brophy Chapel
September 14, 1998

saw a synchronous opportunity to do something special together.

A few days after the September 14 memorial, Jackie and I drove four-and-a-half hours north and checked into the historic El Tovar Hotel. We had dinner that night in the hotel dining room constructed of native stone and Oregon pine, with wall murals representing the customs of four Native American tribes: Hopi, Apache, Mojave and Navajo. The rustic ambiance transported us back in time as we reflected on life, love and loss that year with Jackie's husband Terry in April, and now my husband and her father just months later.

The next morning we donned our hiking boots and descended three-and-a-half hours into the canyon on the Bright Angel Trail. At 64, I was in great shape from all my mornings on the mountain. When we got to the bottom we crossed a bridge spanning the Colorado River and stopped midway. Then we each pulled a small container from our respective backpacks. We had each brought an urn containing our respective husband's ashes. We slowly sprinkled the ashes into the river as the late afternoon sun cast fractured light and shadows. We stood there together talking and reflecting and then made our way to Phantom Ranch, the historic oasis tucked in beside Bright Angel Creek at the bottom of the canyon and only accessible the old-fashioned way: by mule, foot, or raft on the Colorado River. We enjoyed a lovely family dinner at Phantom Ranch with all the other hikers. We were both tired and felt a deep peace that night.

In the morning, after a very early breakfast in the dark, we started the long, grueling climb out on South Kaibab trail. I was physically fit, as was Jackie, but it was still a seven-hour slog to get out of that canyon. In fact, the last half of the climb seemed like an eternity even with Jackie carrying my backpack the last part lest we lose another family member! Overall, it was an exhausting, exhilarating, spiritual and therapeutic time together in remembrance of our lost loved ones. There may not be a more sacred or special place to mark someone's departure from this life and return to the other side.

ONCE I was back in the civilized world, Edward's U.S. senate campaign was a good distraction. As a family, we were all rowing in the same direction. With just weeks until election day, it would be a sprint to the finish. It was an odd time, because we were all still in shock from Ned's recent death and Terry's earlier in the year, and also running in every direction with the campaign. We didn't have time to sit at home and perhaps properly mourn. Instead, we stuffed down our pain and took it on the road. On a campaign trip to Tucson, we realized we were essentially out of campaign funds and any possibility of actually winning had almost entirely faded. This was all about pride and finishing strong despite the odds.

"Mom, we just don't have any money left for this campaign," Edward told me on the way to Tucson.

"There's a reason for everything," I told Edward. I reminded him that the campaign had allowed him to spend most of 1997 and 1998 traveling the state with his father. Not to mention the run-in with the warden south of the border. One of Edward's unusual approaches had been towing his Harley Davidson motorcycle—replete with an Arizona state flag paint job that caused quite a stir at every stop—on a trailer behind the Suburban. Then on campaign stops he'd put Ned on back and zip around town with him, on two wheels. Win or lose, there were many reasons to count our blessings.

On the day of the election, November 3, 1998, we all gathered at Crowne Plaza Hotel to watch the returns come in. The writing was on the wall: Edward did not believe he was going to win. He prepared a brief concession speech that day, made his final campaign stops, ceremoniously cast his own vote and then headed to the hotel.

Indeed, John McCain won his third term to the U.S. Senate. Republicans retained control of both chambers of Congress, although Bill Clinton's party gained seats in the House of Representatives. Edward called McCain to concede and congratulate him. McCain was gracious in victory, and he and Edward would keep in touch in the

"You're only here for a short visit.
Don't hurry, don't worry. And be sure
to smell the flowers along the way."

–Walter Hagen

coming years. We all felt proud of Edward's effort and considered it a success. Despite an official loss, it felt like a victory in many other ways. He'd run as fast and as hard as he could, and did it with honor. He ran a U.S. Senate campaign on his own terms, with almost no money, staffed entirely by his family. And he'd taken his father and brother for a joyride south of the border where they'd broken a man out of a Mexican jail. All in the name of public service, the greater good... and the potential media frenzy that never materialized.

AS 1998 wound down, I sold the Briarwood V house in December. I was now alone, with my husband gone and all the children out of the house. It was an adjustment to a new life. Having my own place for this next chapter seemed like the right thing to do. I moved to the Pavilions on Camelback Road at 36th Street and rented a condominium.

On December 18, 1998, Edward and I attended a members' holiday party at the Camelback Inn Spa. There was a psychic hired to offer free tarot-card readings. The woman studied my cards and told me that I had a year coming up, 1999, that I would not believe. She told me that my entire life would be turned upside down, in a very good way, with a lot of traveling involved. Seven days later her prescience proved correct.

Part III

ONWARD

Back row: Peter, Edward, Patrick.
Sitting: Julie, me, Jackie.

— Chapter Ten —

TELL ME ABOUT YOUR LIFE

"DO YOU PLAY BRIDGE?"

I heard that question in Ixtapa, Mexico, at the Club Med resort playground nestled adjacent to its quaint neighbor town Zihuatanejo. This was another trip Ned and I had planned before his passing, which was to take the entire family to Club Med to close out 1998 and celebrate the New Year. After talking with my five children, we decided Ned would have wanted us to go. We arrived December 23 without the family patriarch, and stayed through January 2.

One day during that trip I was sitting on some bleachers watching my twin 7-year-old grandchildren, Grace Ann and Tommy, performing acrobatics in a mini rodeo arena. I felt a tap on my shoulder. I turned to see an affable man who had walked up and asked me the question about whether I played bridge. When I answered in the affirmative, he added, "I've got one person if you'd like to join us, and I will try to find a fourth." I said I would. Indeed, several days later I began joining Ward and two others for daily bridge sessions. During that same trip,

I also met his two daughters and their children. I did not realize then that this chance meeting was the beginning of the whirlwind year the psychic had foretold at the tarot-card reading.

WARD Rorabeck Munson was a sporting goods magnate and philanthropist. He helped organize the Word War II Japanese surrender ceremony aboard the U.S. battleship *Missouri*. It was on September 2, 1945, that the U.S. Navy lieutenant directed the participants, with now-vaunted historical names, into their positions for the ceremony, including General Douglas MacArthur and Fleet Admiral Chester W. Nimitz. Prior to that, Ward had earned a college degree in rhetoric at UC Berkeley in 1932, at the height of the Great Depression. Unable to find a professional job, he worked construction and at a gas station, and then hopped a train to Chicago to sell orange juice at the 1933 Chicago World's Fair, six years before I would venture to the New York version of the same grand event with my father. Ward eventually landed a sales job with Procter & Gamble and then later, with his wife, Alice, started Munson Sporting Goods, a wholesale business that he moved to Costa Mesa, California, in 1972. When he sold the company in 1981 he stayed on as board chairman. By then, he had built the business into the leading wholesale distributor of outdoor recreational equipment in ten Western states. From the time he sold his company until he asked me if I played bridge, Ward dedicated himself to philanthropy, with the pledge to donate half his wealth. In the 1980s and 1990s he endowed scholarships, built a chapel and donated to numerous colleges, youth programs and rescue missions. Beyond writing checks, Ward often stepped in to volunteer his own time, whether serving food to the homeless or helping organization leaders make effective administrative decisions. By the time we met in Mexico, he was a widower.

As we played cards, Ward shared tidbits of his personal philosophy: *The more you give, the more you get. The more you laugh, the less you*

*fret. The more you do unselfishly, the more you live abundantly. The
more of everything you share, the more you'll always have to share.
The more you love, the more you'll find that life is good and friends
are kind. For only what you give away enriches you from day to day.*

Ward took a sincere interest in other people, and he made the
simple request that opened this memoir: Tell me about your life.
That statement of inquiry encapsulated who he was, a man of great
wealth and influence who genuinely cared for others and wanted to
understand who you were and how you experienced the world. He
was an impressive person who exuded a wholesome goodness, and we
exchanged phone numbers.

With Edward's foray into the political world behind us, the U.S.
Senate trial in the impeachment of President Bill Clinton began January
7, 1999. Interesting to consider that my son would have been seated
for that historic event had he prevailed over John McCain. More than
a month later, the members of the Senate voted to acquit the president.

In early February, Ward's daughter called me and told me her father
would like to come visit me. I asked her to have him call me. When
Ward called, we made arrangements. He came to visit the following
week. He stayed at the Royal Palms Hotel, and we had dinner together
two consecutive nights.

On March 7, Jackie married Bob Hutt—who had been a longtime
friend of Terry Flood—on top of San Sophia in Telluride, Colorado.
Then Ward called again to invite me to go with him to his annual
family reunion in Hawaii in March. I was reticent, because it had only
been six months since we had said goodbye to Ned. I talked with my
children, and they encouraged me to go. I called Ward and said I'd be
happy to go as long he could arrange for us to have separate rooms.

The psychic had nailed it: The trip to Hawaii began a whirlwind
year with a globe-trotting philanthropist who worked with World
Relief and Rotary International. Soon we went on an Asian tour to
Cambodia, South Korea, Malaysia, Singapore, Vietnam and Thailand.
At each stop dignitaries from World Relief met us at the airport and
literally rolled out the red carpet.

Shady

On April 7, I welcomed my fifth grandchild, Gabrielle Kempton Ranger, Patrick's second daughter. On May 14 I experienced my first earthquake while in Palm Desert with Ward, which was a 7.1 doozy. At the end of May, Ward and I left for a three-week trip to South America where again, in Santiago, Chile, while on the sixteenth floor of a Hyatt hotel, Ward and I felt the building swaying during an earthquake. Back in California on June 25, I experienced my third earthquake while at a wedding in Sonoma. Three earthquakes in six weeks!

On July 10, Brandi Chastain of the U.S. women's national soccer team scored the game-winning penalty kick against China in the FIFA Women's World Cup. Whether you were a soccer fan or not, that photograph of her on her knees celebrating was unforgettable. That same month, another tragedy struck on the evening of July 16, when John F. Kennedy Jr., son of the presidential candidate I had seen in person in Michigan in 1960, died while piloting his aircraft near Martha's Vineyard, Massachusetts. Also on board were his wife Carolyn Bessette and her sister Lauren Bessette, who both perished, too. It brought to mind, for me, those wonderful flights with my

father in his small plane and how naive I was as a child to the inherent dangers of aviation, especially in small aircraft. My memories of our adventures into the clear blue were only of adrenaline, wholesome fun and bonding time with my father.

That autumn, on November 20, I married Ward Munson, 89, who was twenty-four years my senior. My daughter Julie and son-in-law Tom hosted the wedding dinner at their house. We had a family breakfast the next morning at the Royal Palms Hotel.

To close out the year, I took Ward and the entire family on a Christmas Celebrity Cruise in December. Our start and end point was San Juan, Puerto Rico. From there we headed south to lush tropical landscapes, with our first port of call Charlotte Amalie, the enchanting capital of St. Thomas. What a joy it was to stroll this quaint island paradise that has drawn pirates and sailors for centuries. Our next stop was St. Kitts, a blend of French and English colonial architecture with more breathtaking beaches and mountain peaks. Then it was off to Antigua, which Christopher Columbus named in 1493. Stops in St. Lucia and Barbados capped off the highlights before we cruised back to San Juan to disembark and return to the mainland.

As the 1990s ended and we welcomed a new century with the year 2000, we were all grateful the world did not devolve into chaos as many had predicted, with the Y2K frenzy and the fear that all the computers would go berserk.

ON February 12, 2000, the creator of the *Peanuts* comic strip Charles Schulz died, with his final original strip published the next day. I had enjoyed *Peanuts* my entire life, with the first collection of strips published in 1952 when I was working for Rudolph Leitman New York Life Insurance in the First National Bank building in Detroit. Unbelievably, at its peak *Peanuts* appeared daily in 2,600 newspapers in seventy-five countries, in twenty-one languages. Including merchandise and product endorsements, Charlie Brown and company produced revenues of more than $1 billion each year, with the creator Schulz earning some $40 million annually. Facts I learned about Schulz seemed to mirror my own life philosophies, which were to enjoy life, follow your passions and keep moving. During the long run of *Peanuts*, Schulz only took only one vacation, a five-week break in 1997 to celebrate his 75th birthday. And what American hasn't seen the first animated TV special, *A Charlie Brown Christmas*, which my children dutifully watched every year since it first aired in December 1965.

ON April 29, I welcomed my sixth grandchild, and first of the new century, Julia Mercier Hutt. Ward and I traveled to South America again, from May 29 to June 18, another spiritual experience as I watched Ward dedicate himself to helping others. Our routine included spending most of July at his place in Tahoe City, Nevada. In August we visited his daughter Rosemary and son-in-law Jim Tracy on Bainbridge Island, Washington, a locale that requires a ferry ride from Seattle. We were back on Bainbridge Island for the week of Thanksgiving and then in sunny Arizona for Christmas with my children. My children knew I had found a good man in Ward, whose joy in life was giving to others and leaving behind a legacy of giving through his foundation.

On October 19, my seventh grandchild, Barbara Shea Adelson, was born. Ward and I had been living in Palm Springs since getting married, but we subsequently moved back to Arizona, to the Sun City Grand neighborhood. Our house was at 15119 West Alegria Court in Surprise.

Julie (L), Bobbie, me, Julia and Jackie.

The 2000 U.S. presidential election between George W. Bush and Al Gore was a real mess when the U.S. Supreme Court prevented the Florida Secretary of State from certifying the election results, which allowed recounting to continue for weeks. It wasn't all resolved until December 12 when the high court, in *Bush v. Gore*, overturned a ruling by the Florida Supreme Court, which ended the recount, granted Florida's electoral votes to Bush and led to Gore conceding. This would not be the last election in which the Democratic candidate would receive more votes and lose the election; it would happen again in 2016 by an even wider margin.

*"To know how to grow old is the
masterwork of wisdom, and one of
the most difficult chapters in the great
art of living."*

–Henri Frédéric Ariel

With all that unfolding, Ward and I took refuge in family time and followed the same holiday schedule: Thanksgiving with Ward's daughter on Bainbridge Island and Christmas with the Rangers in Arizona. When we weren't traveling, Ward and I spent Wednesdays at the Westside Food Bank serving the homeless.

In 2001, my grandchildren Julia and Barbara got baptized on February 18 at that ever-present locale of so many family milestones, Brophy College Chapel. In June, Ward and I spent time in Durango at Jackie and Bob's place and then went to Tahoe City again for the month of July. From September 28 to October 12, Ward and I were in Canada. The seminal event of 2001 was, of course, the terrorist attacks on September 11. I had the television on that morning and thought it was a movie. Then Patrick called me and asked if I'd seen what was happening.

IN 2002, Ward and I took a Panama Canal cruise from April 7 to 17. Then on April 26 we were at Tuccetti's in Scottsdale on a rainy evening for a rehearsal dinner. My son Edward had met Esthela Thayde Borbón Baltazar in Mexico, and now he had come home with her to get married. The wedding took place at 3 p.m. the next day at The Old Church at All Saints Catholic Newman Center, followed by a reception at the University Club in Tempe.

My son Patrick welcomed his son Patrick McDonald Ranger, his first son and third child—and my eighth grandchild—on May 23. In July, Ward and I spent time again in Tahoe City and then went to a Munson family reunion in Seattle August 1 through 4. In late September we left Boston on a cruise that wound north through Novia Scotia, Halifax, Prince Edward Island and Bar Harbor. On November 7 we left for what would be the last great act of benevolence in Ward's life, a Rotary International mission to China.

PEACE
on earth

Ward & Sandy Munson
Great Wall of China
November 10, 2002

— Chapter Eleven —

THE MORE YOU LOVE

TWENTY MINUTES INTO THE FLIGHT, just as we were settling in for the next sixteen hours, Ward knew something was wrong.

"Do you have one of those nitroglycerin pills?" he said, a serious look of discomfort etched on his face. We were sitting in aisle seats across from each other. I hurriedly gave him the small white pill, and before I could screw the cap back on the plastic bottle, my husband's chin was on his chest. His face went slack. Trying not to panic, I immediately pressed the call button. A flight attendant put out a call on the speaker asking if there was a doctor aboard: There were five. The doctors carried Ward into the third galley and began working on him as I waited, feeling helpless.

We had just spent eight days in China. We'd arrived in the capital city of Beijing on Saturday, November 9. We'd visited Shanghai and Hangzhou. We'd walked atop the Great Wall of China and toured the Ming Tombs. We visited the centuries-old Lingyin Temple with its sixty-four foot camphor wood Buddha carving. I saw silk being embroidered, a 1,000-year-old craft, at the National Embroidery Institute. The day before we left we wandered through the Yu Garden, a peaceful maze of marvelous pavilions, pods, rock works and arching trees. Even at 92, Ward had no physical issues our entire trip or throughout our marriage. Ever since we had married, I had always gone with Ward to his physical checkups. His doctor had told him to always carry a bottle of nitroglycerin tablets, which he did due to a heart condition. We even took one last swim together in the hotel pool before our scheduled return to Los Angeles, on November 16, 2002.

"Those pool attendants were so nice," he said that morning. "But I forgot to tip them." He left the room to give the attendants each a handsome tip.

Hours later we were aboard the airplane; we were in the first row behind the third galley, in the aisle seats. Forty-five minutes after a flight attendant had summoned the doctors aboard the aircraft, Ward Munson died. The doctors carefully placed his body in a lavatory and draped a blue blanket over the door. I was in shock, numb and deeply saddened. The captain of the flight crew came to talk to me and explain the vagaries of international law regarding deceased passengers.

"I will do whatever you want," he said. "However, if we land in China, or perhaps Japan, with a deceased person, it will be a long bureaucratic process and a lot of paperwork before you'll be able to leave with him. You may be stuck wherever we land for days trying to sort this out."

Meanwhile, back stateside, a ringing phone jolted my youngest son, who was sound asleep at 3 a.m. When he answered, he heard a thick foreign accent ask, "Is this Peter Ranger?"

"Yes."

"Are you Ward Munson's son?"

Well, no, Peter thought. But he also knew I had asked before the trip if I could list him as my emergency contact, so he made the connection and simply said, "Yes."

"He's dead."

Click. Dial tone. Peter was left stunned and unsure what it all meant—and whether I, too, was injured or worse. Ward's daughter Rosemary received a similarly haunting call with few details. Neither had any way to reach Ward or me.

Back on the airplane, we were still over mainland China. Or diverting southeast to Japan was another option. I talked with all of Ward's close friends from Rotary International who had accompanied us on the trip. We all unanimously agreed that it would be best to proceed nonstop to Los Angeles and land on American soil to avoid a legal morass. Those next sixteen hours were the most anxious and fitful I have ever experienced. The mental image of Ward's body slumped in an airplane lavatory haunted me throughout the flight and for a long time afterward. When we landed in Los Angeles, with all the flashing lights and first responders, it was like arriving on a crime scene.

Inside the terminal, my sons Patrick and Peter were waiting for me. Since my family had my itinerary, Patrick and Peter had decided to meet me in Los Angeles. They waited as Ward's friends from Rotary International helped arrange transport of Ward's body to a local mortuary. Per his express wishes, he would be cremated. By the time we'd sorted it all out, I'd been up fifty straight hours and was an emotional wreck, just four days shy of what would have been our third wedding anniversary. I had a pit in my stomach and couldn't fully process what had just happened. Eventually I was on another airplane, with my two sons, for the final leg from Los Angeles to Phoenix, my mind and emotions in a blur. At some point during that flight it hit me that I was now alone again, at least in marriage. But I was never truly alone as I walked into the terminal at Sky Harbor Airport, with two of my sons by my side and my daughters Jackie and Julie waiting for us.

IN January 2003, armed sky marshals begin appearing on U.S. airlines in an attempt to prevent hijackings. It was another reminder that life after 9/11 was irrevocably altered. In my corner of the world, on April 18, 2003, my ninth grandchild, Sandra Devina Ranger, was born to my

"Kindness is more important than wisdom, and the recognition of this is the beginning of wisdom."

–Theodore Isaac Rubin

son Edward and Esthella; she was named after both her grandmothers. By the following summer I was the newly widowed 69-year-old asking that vital question: What did I want to do with my life? As I shared earlier, some of my yoga instructors had the answer: that I would be a great yoga instructor.

After my grand and life-changing Bikram Yoga experiment in California and getting certified as an instructor, I bought my own house on a cold morning in January 2004. I would move in May 6, into the Casa Blanca community in Scottsdale, which would lead to me getting invited to a party where I would meet the woman who had founded the Casa Blanca Book Club in 1994. Soon I would be invited to join, which was the first seed to starting to write this memoir twenty-five years later in 2019. The day before I moved into Casa Blanca, I celebrated a special milestone: my tenth grandchild, Stella Esperanza Ranger, who was fittingly born on Cinco de Mayo (May 5) to her Mexican mother Esthela and bilingual American father Edward, the former longshot candidate for the U.S. Senate.

Living in Casa Blanca in 2004 also led me to cross paths with a neighbor, Bob Baeder, when he was out getting his newspaper one morning. Two years later we were married, on April 8, 2006. I moved into his unit in Casa Blanca. For me, the third time was definitely not the charm. By November 2015 our divorce was final and, thankfully, I was able to come full circle and move back to unit 204, where I have lived to the present day and plan to be until the end. Robert Walter Baeder passed away April 21, 2016.

In 2008, Edward McDonald Ranger III was born November 14 in Mexico City to Esthela and Edward. He was my eleventh grandchild. In 2010, I welcomed my twelfth grandchild, Michael Joseph Ranger, who was also born in Mexico City, on November 18, to Esthela and Edward. In 2013, my lucky thirteenth grandchild, Hattie Violet Mayes, was born May 16. She is the daughter of my son Peter Ranger and Kris Mayes.

All of us wearing our "Snady"shirts at the El Tovar Hotel.

In 2014, to celebrate my 80th birthday, I hiked to the bottom of the Grand Canyon for a second time—and towed along my entire immediate family. We all stayed at the historic El Tovar Hotel again and then Phantom Ranch, just as Jackie and I had when we said goodbye to our first husbands. In 2015, after living in Mexico City since 2008, Edward and Esthela moved back to Arizona with their four children.

Santiago de Compostela.

— Chapter Twelve —

THE POWER OF PILGRIMAGE

EVER SINCE I HAD WATCHED *The Way*, a 2010 film featuring Martin Sheen and his son Emilio Estevez, the idea of making the traditional Spanish pilgrimage "El Camino de Santiago," or "The Way of St. James" in English, had been number one on my bucket list (tied for first with "Write my memoir"). In the film, the father character travels to Spain to recover the body of his estranged son, played by Estevez, who died while traveling the Camino de Santiago route. The father decides to take the pilgrimage himself. The Camino de Santiago is actually a network of different ancient pilgrim routes stretching across Europe and coming together at the tomb of St. James in Santiago de Compostela in northwest Spain. The film was a powerful and inspirational story about family, friends and the challenges we each face in this journey of life.

In 2016 I decided it was time to fulfill the dream of making my own pilgrimage, and further decided it would be great fun if both my daughters, Julie and Jackie, would do it with me. I contacted Fresco Tours in Bilbao, Spain, and requested an itinerary of their 2016 guided tours. I then had to check that schedule against Julie and Jackie's availability and, unfortunately, there was not a date that worked for all three of us. Jackie and I ended up settling on the kinder Camino de Santiago trip May 4 to 14. Meanwhile, Julie and her family had already scheduled a European trip during the same time, so she would at least be on the same continent. Interestingly, my son Peter had walked the entire 500-mile Camino de Santiago route, from Saint Jean Pied de Port, France, through four of Spain's fifteen regions, and ending in Galicia, Spain.

Jackie and I took an American Airlines flight from Phoenix to Philadelphia on May 1, and then continued on from Philadelphia to Madrid. We checked into the NH Paseo del Prado Madrid hotel, which was the official accommodation for our group and the starting point for our trek. On our first morning, after a nice breakfast in the hotel, Jackie and I saw on TV that the Madrid Open Tennis Tournament was being played and decided to take the Metro to the stadium. Once there, we bought amazing seats—center court, first row—from which we watched our favorite tennis player, Rafael Nadal, win his quarterfinal match in his native country. What a thrill! When we got back to our hotel we were summoned to the lobby, where we gathered with our seven fellow tour group members. We already knew our very good friend Nan, from Scottsdale, who introduced two of her best friends, Jill from St. Louis and Barb from Boston. Completing the group were Jen from New York, Jan from Idaho, and Kay and Edward from Texas.

On the appointed start day, Wednesday, May 4, we all met in the lobby. Our guides, Ana and Roberto, were both from Spain and explained what would be happening on our eighty-mile tour. We would be making one of the holiest Christian pilgrimages, which has been a route for more than 1,000 years. Earlier believers thought this ancient route followed through the Milky Way Galaxy to what people believed at the time was the end of the Earth. We traveled that day by private bus, making several historic stops on the way. As we had done almost twenty years earlier, in September 1998 when we hiked down into the Grand Canyon, Jackie and I had each brought some of our respective husbands' ashes to sprinkle at different historic spots along our journey. We spent our first night at the Real Colegiata in Leon.

The scallop shell and yellow arrow are the symbols of the Camino de Santiago, and these markings would guide us all the way to Santiago de Compostela. The scallop shell is believed to be a metaphor, its lines representing the different routes the pilgrims travel from all over the world, all trails leading to one point: Santiago de Compostela. The yellow arrow shows pilgrims the way along the Camino de Santiago.

On the second day we went by van to Rabanal, visiting the Iron

Cross where pilgrims leave a stone to ask for protection while on their journey. Jackie and I both brought stones from home, which our priest had blessed at our church before leaving. We also sprinkled the first of our respective stash of ashes here. We stayed two nights at the Hotel Alfonso IX in Sarria. On Day Three we visited ruins and the Benedictine Monastery in Samos.

One of the highlights of the trip came every afternoon, around 2 p.m., when we would stop for a late lunch at some of the most quaint restaurants I've encountered. As a group, we would enjoy a family-style meal fit for kings and queens. Then some more hiking and, after arriving back at the hotel, we had time to take a shower and enjoy another wonderful meal, a late dinner at either the hotel or a local restaurant. Good thing there were no scales in our rooms throughout that trip! To help offset the calorie load, Jackie had mentioned to our group that I was a Bikram Yoga instructor. The group nominated me, at 82 years old, to lead a twenty-minute yoga class every day, which at least gave us the illusion that we would not gain weight on this trip.

It was on Day Four that we began walking, with the first leg to Portomarín. After lunch, the path took us through farmland, woods and into the agricultural hamlet of Gondar. We spent the next two nights at the Pousada de Portomarín hotel. The next day we walked back in time from Gondar to Palas de Rei, stopping at many churches and the 17th century Cross of Lameiros.

Day Six was a beautiful walk up and down rolling hills along quiet footpaths. The weather was perfect, with temperatures in the sixties and intermittent sprinkles of rain that had us donning and then shedding our rain ponchos every thirty minutes. We arrived in Melide, where street vendors boiled octopus in large copper kettles. We would stay in Arzua at the Pazo Santa Maria hotel for the next three nights.

On Day Seven we left Melide and ventured into the Galician countryside, dotted with so many beautiful churches. Day Eight brought more wonderful scenery in the Galician countryside. We met lots of local people and villagers who happily greeted us with "Hola." On that day we felt a shift, that we were no longer just tourists but

"A tree that reaches past your embrace grows from one small seed. A structure over nine stories high begins with a handful of earth. A journey of a thousand miles starts with a single step."

–Tao Te Ching (paraphrase)

rather pilgrims on El Camino de Santiago.

Day Nine was an excursion to the Santa Maria Monastery of Sobrado, where the monks welcomed us. Then we walked to Lavacolla, where in the Middle Ages weary pilgrims would wash themselves before entering the holy city of Santiago, our destination the next day. Sleep that night at the Ruta Jacobea Hotel was a bit fitful, with the anticipation building as we approached the culmination of our journey.

On Friday, May 13, our excitement as weary travelers was palpable. Although Jackie and I had both brought ashes to sprinkle, our concept of quantity had differed greatly. Jackie had appropriately brought about three tablespoons, which she could easily store, carry and sprinkle discreetly without issue. For whatever reason, my son Edward had given me a very large bag of ashes. So, although I had been sprinkling Ned's remains all along the way, by the last day my bag was still very full. Jackie and I were sitting at a very large fountain, and I asked her what I should do. She looked around, and not seeing many people, suggested I slowly pour them into the fountain, which I did. Except the fountain started to completely foam up. We discreetly slipped away, wondering what local ordinances I'd probably just violated.

Our group (that's me, third from the right).

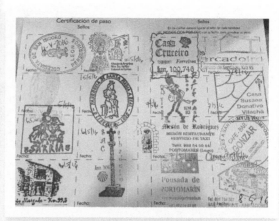

What a feeling it was that day to walk through the busy town center and then arrive at the Santiago de Compostela Cathedral. Our group converged there with other travelers from all over the world, with many hands held aloft and tears filling eyes. We requested and retrieved our certificates from the office, officially declaring the completion of our pilgrimage while it poured rain. No one seemed to mind, as we were all shouting, clapping and forming celebratory circles. I still cherish the videotape of this scene provided by Fresco Tours. After the celebration we went to Hotel Virxe de Cerca and, after showers, got ready to go to the pilgrims' mass before dinner.

It took my breath away when I walked into Santiago de Compostela Cathedral and went to the spot where I kissed the stone feet of a statue of St. James, which was followed by a wonderful mass. Jackie and I felt especially blessed to witness one of the most famous symbols of the cathedral, the Botafumeiro, a swinging "smoke expeller" for burning incense, because no Catholic mass is complete without good special effects! This famous thurible weighs some 116 pounds. Using a system of pulleys, it swings from the central cupola of the cathedral, taking eight people to hoist it to a suspended height of sixty-five feet, where it reaches speeds of more than forty miles per hour. One tradition has it that the use of a swinging censor in the Santiago de Compostela Cathedral began in the eleventh century for arriving pilgrims who were tired and unwashed. The belief was that the incense smoke had a protective effect during that time of plagues and epidemics. After this wonderful celebration we returned to the hotel for our final late-night celebratory dinner. We truly had formed a bond with each person in our group and our two guides. On Saturday, May 14, we reluctantly said our last "buen camino" after breakfast. Jackie and I stayed an extra night and returned to Phoenix via London on May 16.

The year 2016 was a tumultuous one in the long run-up to one of the most divisive, vitriolic and ugly national elections in our nation's history. What struck me during those days in Spain was the feeling of solidarity we had lost as Americans as our political discourse devolved into a binary cultural war: us against them, red states versus blue states and Republican versus Democrat. Walking "El Camino" was so pleasant, and surprising, because of the wholehearted camaraderie and solidarity that existed among the pilgrims. We enjoyed a bubble of unity as we simply followed a long tradition that still remains, the spirit of the pilgrim that leads to helping and uplifting each other rather than retreating into our warring factions.

It is my hope that one day we can reclaim that spirit in America, similar to the immediate aftermath of September 11, 2001—perhaps the last time we were truly united as one nation, under God, and indivisible despite our differences.

Julie, Peter, Edward, me, Jackie and Patrick.

— Epilogue —

AUTUMN 2020

"TELL ME ABOUT YOUR LIFE."

When I was a little girl I wanted to be a gymnast. I did have a gymnastics class in high school, but I never did become a gymnast. I became something better: mother to five children. Together with Ned, we raised and shepherded those children the best we could into adulthood. That journey included a cross-country move, from Michigan to Arizona, which was the best thing we ever did. We began that journey together, Ned and I, but he passed on and left me to cross the finish line on my own. Ned will always be my first true love, the father of my children.

My time with Ward Munson changed the way I look at things. He gave so much and was so unselfish. I think it was largely his influence that led me into my own spiritual discovery through yoga and the weirdness of Bikram Choudhury and his obsession with six-figure vintage cars. In that way, I would say Ward Munson changed my life with his goodness, because there was a palpable benevolence radiating from that man. I too wanted to share goodness.

Shady

In school I was a decent student. But I think I was more street-smart than school-smart, growing up mostly fatherless and learning my way in Detroit. And in the last two decades of my life especially, in my late sixties, seventies and into my eighties, I've delved more into good books because reading takes you places. I love it. And that's what led me to meet a talented author named Landon J. Napoleon, and eventually an unlikely idea began to form: to pen my own memoir starting at 85 years old.

I love to tell stories. In my next life I'd like to become a good motivational speaker. I'm grateful that I've taken the time to sit down and capture these snapshots of my life, the best I can remember, for my children, their spouses, my grandchildren and their children to one day read.

Do I have regrets? No, I regret nothing. I made my choices and decisions and steps—and missteps— in life, doing the best I could with the information I had at the time. Instead of regret I've always fallen back on my sense of humor. Learning to laugh at oneself has served me well.

I've been lucky in love and lucky in life. I've won the life lottery in so many ways, with my husband Ned, our children and grandchildren, and the special time I had with Ward Munson. Together I witnessed all his charity as we traveled to some twenty-five countries.

I have what I think is a bit of ESP, some sort of extrasensory perception that allows me to sense things before they happen. If I were dispensing any life advice, I'd keep it simple: Keep a positive attitude and enjoy whatever you're doing.

Be picky: Have a small group of friends and surround yourself with supportive people. Let go of the needy people who will just drain your battery.

Don't burn bridges; they're hard to mend and repair, if not impossible. Take your time and sleep on it. Don't be too quick to say hurtful things. Be kind.

And, of course, age is mind over matter: If you don't mind, it doesn't matter. That belief is what allowed me to become a certified yoga teacher at age 69. And hike to the bottom of the Grand Canyon, twice, including that last time at age 80, and up and down Squaw Peak

*"Learn from the past. Do not come to
the end of your life only to find you have
not lived. For many come to the point of
leaving the space of the earth and when
they gaze back, they see the joy and the
beauty that could not be theirs because of
the fears they lived."*

–Clearwater

more times than I can count (in total darkness, no less). To that end, my travels have continued to this day.

Over the last decade, my youngest son Peter (my only unmarried child) and I have been on numerous small excursions, domestic trips and international jaunts. Our travels started in 2008, when Peter moved to Miami Beach to work for a hospice company. Over the next five years I would travel south to visit Peter at least once a year. After Peter left this company he decided to travel the world, and eventually wrote a book, *Actively Dying*, which is still a work in progress, that includes Peter's observations from a decade working in hospice care—where he came to understand death—and his five-year, peripatetic journey to uncover answers about life. Perhaps, like me, he'll finish it when he's 86!

Another stop on Peter's travels was New York City. Again, this was a wonderful place for me to visit at least once a year during the various seasons. In early 2017 I was researching cruises, and one that particularly caught my eye was a *New York Times* journalist transatlantic crossing on the Queen Mary 2, embarking from Brooklyn and disembarking in Southampton, England. I asked Peter if he would be interested. It was limited to a small group, as there would be various daily classes taught by the five journalists. After classes we enjoyed cocktail parties and formal dinners. We took the cruise in July, spent some time in London, and then went on to Portugal for a few weeks. In December of that same year I went back to New York to spend New Year's Eve with Peter, and then we traveled to Rhode Island, New Hampshire and Vermont during a polar vortex that required us to use hand and toe warmers because it was so bitter cold. In July 2018 Peter and I spent a month exploring the entire state of Maine. In July 2019 we took the Queen Mary 2 transatlantic crossing from Brooklyn to Southampton once more, again spending a couple weeks in London and then moving onto to Cork, Ireland, where we visited Blarney Castle.

Above, that's me kissing the Blarney Stone.

In March 2020 Peter moved back to Miami Beach, while I've pretty much been hunkered down in quarantine working on my book. During 2020 I did get to spend two weeks in Coeur d' Alene, Idaho, in June and then four weeks in Coronado, California.

I am blessed to be so loved by all of my thirteen grandchildren, who each express their love to me directly. I am in regular contact with each of them, and we share unique, incredible bonds. So how fitting it was that, in 2018, one of my granddaughters wrote a speech for a college course that seemed to capture the special bond I share with all my grandchildren. In other words, it was as though Julia Mercier Hutt, a freshman at University of Colorado in Boulder at the time, put into words what all my grandchildren believe. Her words beautifully captured who I am, my connection to my family and how the title of this memoir came to be.

Our Grandmother

Have you ever felt a tight bond to someone or something, where you know you could never live without them? Well, this bond that I have is with my amazing, caring and funny grandma. Second only to my immediate family, my connection with my grandmother is a relationship like no other.

My grandmother and I text every day and exchange our favorite emojis: hers is the dancing man who goes like this, and we tell stories nonstop. Now, this woman is no ordinary grandmother. If anything, she may be hipper than my friends and I combined.

My cousins and I call her "Grandma Snady" instead of her real name, Sandy. Now, this nickname came to be when she was at a business convention, and the man writing her nametag switched the "a" and the "n." The whole night she walked around with this name tag, with strangers calling her Snady. She shared this story with all of us, and soon the name stuck. She even has a personalized "Snady" license plate on her car, which makes it very easy to spot her going 25 in a 50 mile-per-hour zone.

Grandma Snady is not your average grandma who enjoys cats and needlepointing. She is a certified Bikram yoga instructor and swims a mile of backstroke every single day. When I call to check in on her, she will answer the phone and ask me about my day and so on, but once I ask her about her day, she will go off on a tangent: "Well, Julia, I have had a day. I've been up since 4 a.m., had brunch with JoAnn Stewart, shopped a bit and went to the bank, but I am so exhausted I need to put on my PJs and go to bed. See ya' later!" Then she hangs up.

Like any other grandma, she has her obsessions. One, in particular, is her obsession with Butterfinger candy bars. Every Halloween, ever since I was old enough to trick-or-treat, I would catch her at our house going through my pillowcase looking for Butterfinger bars. Like,

Grandma, all you had to do was ask. She also loves her beer with ice, and always has her frozen powdered-sugar mini-donuts.

I am her go-to for all things technology, whether it is her mail app disappearing, photos being blurry, or have you seen my phone? Well, Grandma, you're calling me, so maybe look in your hand? She is on Facebook, Instagram and Bumble—yes, you heard that right: I even helped her set up an account on Bumble. She has outlived her three husbands. All right, Grandma Snady, let's put you on a dating app!

We will sit for hours and hours playing gin rummy and talking about our family drama. Whose ideal 80th birthday celebration is hiking into and back out of the Grand Canyon? You guessed it! Grandma Snady.

My bond with my grandma has grown stronger and stronger as I have matured. What else could I ask for? Our bond is quite unique. Not even my own mom, Grandma's daughter Jackie, totally gets it. I can confide in Grandma about anything, and she tells me everyone should always have someone to tell their secrets to and know the secrets are safe. She even said: "Let's face it: your parents are a little strict and judgy." You're telling me, Grandma.

Whenever I get a chance, I take her out to breakfast at her favorite place, The Pancake House, and we both indulge in a large Dutch baby, which is a monster pancake with syrup and powdered sugar.

This woman is not only my grandma, but she is my best friend. I know that may sound cheesy, but it's the truth. Most of my friends dread spending time with their grandparents, but I look forward to every minute I have with her.

Every time I see her in a new Eileen Fisher outfit, it brings a smile to my face. She truly just gets me, and I get her. She is the wisest, funniest and most caring person I have ever met. She'll call you out for your bullshit, and also pull you aside to keep you from being yelled at by your parents.

As Cecelia Ahern once said, "Age is just a number," and she has never been more right.

There were two other big "grandchildren" events in the Ranger family in 2018: a U.S. Marine NROTC commissioning ceremony for my grandson, second lieutenant Jack Hutt, at the University of Wisconsin in Madison, on May 12, and the marriage of my granddaughter Grace Ann Adelson (my namesake) on September 15 in Coeur d'Alene, Idaho. On May 30, 2020, my granddaughter Caroline Palmer Ranger married in Paradise Valley, Arizona.

In fact, each of my thirteen grandchildren are unique and loving in their own ways, and so good to their grandma. I am so blessed to have them all!

THANK you for coming along on this journey with me that begin in 1934 and includes writing this book through the unprecedented events of 2020: a global coronavirus pandemic—from one death in the United States in February to more than 200,000 before year's end—the death of George Floyd and the long-overdue uprising calling for equal justice for African Americans. If 2020 has demonstrated anything, it's that none of us knows what the future holds.

I do believe in God. I thank God every morning when I wake up. I have lived a blessed life. I am the luckiest person in the whole world. I love my family, and I know they love me. I think in the end, if there is one takeaway I'd like to leave you with after reading this memoir, it would be this: There is nothing greater than the love we share with our family and friends. Beyond anything else—whether accumulating a vast fortune or piling up accomplishments—it is the invaluable bond of our loved ones that is the most important thing to build, protect and cherish in life. In that way, as the global pandemic has blindsided us all, I have been able to retreat to the safety, love and comfort of my children, my grandchildren and their families. There is not a greater gift you can give yourself in this lifetime: the love of family.

Mine started in 1954, when my life intersected with Edward McDonald Ranger at a holiday party in Detroit. Who could have known that sixty-five years after that innocent introduction, I would begin putting down the memories of a lifetime with that man, our five children, our thirteen grandchildren and the attendant highs and lows of this chosen life. It's almost incomprehensible to consider all that has transpired. I am humbled by my many blessings, and beyond grateful for the life I have lived. I would say the following quotation sums it all up better than I ever could:

To laugh often and much; to win the respect of intelligent people and the affection of children; to earn the appreciation of honest critics and endure the betrayal of false friends. To appreciate beauty; to find the best in others; to leave the world a bit better whether by a healthy child, a garden patch or a redeemed social condition; to know that even one life has breathed easier because you have lived. This is to have succeeded.
—Ralph Waldo Emerson (1803-1882)

My grandson Jack.

— How to make it —

TO 86 AND BEYOND...

WELL, HELLO! IF YOU'RE STILL READING you're probably someone who stays to watch all the film credits. This page is that little bonus scene you get by sticking around to the very end.

I'd like to include some personal facts about my life and longevity, which I get asked about almost on a daily basis. To say that I'm a little OCD is certainly not an overstatement. I am a neatnik and very focused. Always have been and always will be. Have those traits helped me live longer? Yes, I believe, because an ordered house and mind reduce stress.

I never miss my comprehensive annual physical and twice-yearly eye doctor appointments, and I visit my dental hygienist four times a year. So, very important: by doing this I'm staying ahead of the game. I call it preventative medicine. For some reason, throughout my life and even more so in my later years, I find people seeking me out for advice (including many of my yoga students). These questions run the gamut, from marriage issues to financial problems and family disputes: I've

193

heard it all. I have one stock reply to any question: "You only have one life to live—is this how you want to live it?"

People also constantly ask how I stay so lean—I'm the same weight as when I married Ned in 1956. My answer: daily exercise and, for the most part, healthy eating. (Notwithstanding my daily frozen, powdered sugar mini-donut). I believe you are whatever you put in your body.

To that end, a typical day for me is rising early and never leaving the bedroom before I make the bed. I do an hour and a half of exercise every morning that has included aerobics classes, hiking, hot yoga and swimming. After exercise I return home and, after a leisurely shower, I make myself a latte (or two) and my usual McCann's Irish oatmeal. I read two newspapers and work four crossword puzzles. I'm still old-fashioned: I still like to hold a newspaper, and books, in my hands. I try not to schedule any appointments before 11 a.m., at which time I am raring to go.

Also, I keep a pen and notepad by my nightstand when going to bed at night, so if I think of something I would like to do the next day I have a place to jot it down. If I didn't do this I don't think I would be able to fall asleep as quickly as I do.

That's another question I get: What time do you go to bed? In giving my answer, like many things I try to incorporate into my life, I keep it simple:

When I am tired.

The time just before dawn contains the most energy of all hours of the day. This has helped me become an early riser and an early doer.

—Terri Guillemets

— About the Authors —

GRACE SANDRA FALL RANGER was born in 1934 in Philadelphia, and in 1939 flew to the World's Fair in New York with her father piloting his own plane. She has lived in Pennsylvania, Michigan and, since 1979, Arizona. She is the mother of five children and has thirteen grandchildren. She has traveled to more than twenty-five countries, experienced three earthquakes on two continents and, at age 69, became certified as a yoga instructor. She has hiked to the bottom of the Grand Canyon twice, including when she was 80 to celebrate her birthday. This is her first book.

LANDON J. NAPOLEON is the award-winning and critically acclaimed author of numerous fiction and nonfiction books that have been translated into multiple foreign editions. He is a previous Barnes & Noble "Discover Great New Writers" finalist, his debut novel *ZigZag* was adapted into a film, and his nonfiction biography *Burning Shield: The Jason Schechterle Story* was a "The Arizona Republic Recommends" selection. He has a bachelor's degree in journalism from Arizona State University and a master's degree in creative writing from University of Glasgow in Scotland. He lives in Arizona.

Made in the USA
Coppell, TX
13 February 2021